Quod scriptura, non iubet vetat

The Latin translates, "What is not commanded in scripture, is forbidden:'

On the Cover: Baptists rejoice to hold in common with other evangelicals the main principles of the orthodox Christian faith. However, there are points of difference and these differences are significant. In fact, because these differences arise out of God's revealed will, they are of vital importance. Hence, the barriers of separation between Baptists and others can hardly be considered a trifling matter. To suppose that Baptists are kept apart solely by their views on Baptism or the Lord's Supper is a regrettable misunderstanding. Baptists hold views which distinguish them from Catholics, Congregationalists, Episcopalians, Lutherans, Methodists, Pentecostals, and Presbyterians, and the differences are so great as not only to justify, but to demand, the separate denominational existence of Baptists. Some people think Baptists ought not teach and emphasize their differences but as E.J. Forrester stated in 1893, "Any denomination that has views which justify its separate existence, is bound to promulgate those views. If those views are of sufficient importance to justify a separate existence, they are important enough to create a duty for their promulgation ... the very same reasons which justify the separate existence of any denomination make it the duty of that denomination to teach the distinctive doctrines upon which its separate existence rests." If Baptists have a right to a separate denominational life, it is their duty to propagate their distinctive principles, without which their separate life cannot be justified or maintained.

Many among today's professing Baptists have an agenda to revise the Baptist distinctives and redefine what it means to be a Baptist. Others don't understand why it even matters. The books being reproduced in the *Baptist Distinctives Series* are republished in order that Baptists from the past may state, explain and defend the primary Baptist distinctives as they understood them. It is hoped that this Series will provide a more thorough historical perspective on what it means to be distinctively Baptist.

The Lord Jesus Christ asked, *"And why call ye me, Lord, Lord, and do not the things which I say?"* (Luke 6:46). The immediate context surrounding this question explains what it means to be a true disciple of Christ. Addressing the same issue, Christ's question is meant to show that a confession of discipleship to the Lord Jesus Christ is inconsistent and untrue if it is not accompanied with a corresponding submission to His authoritative commands. Christ's question teaches us that a true recognition of His authority as Lord inevitably includes a submission to the authority of His Word. Hence, with this question Christ has made it forever impossible to separate His authority as King from the authority of His Word. These two principles—the authority of Christ as King and the authority of His Word—are the two most fundamental Baptist distinctives. The first gives rise to the second and out of these two all the other Baptist distinctives emanate. As F.M. lams wrote in 1894, "Loyalty to Christ as King, manifesting itself in a constant and unswerving obedience to His will as revealed in His written Word, is the real source of all the Baptist distinctives:' In the search for the *primary* Baptist distinctive many have settled on the Lordship of Christ as the most basic distinctive. Strangely, in doing this, some have attempted to separate Christ's Lordship from the authority of Scripture, as if you could embrace Christ's authority without submitting to what He commanded. However, while Christ's Lordship and Kingly authority can be isolated and considered essentially for discussion's sake, we see from Christ's own words in Luke 6:46 that His Lordship is really inseparable from His Word and, with regard to real Christian discipleship, there can be no practical submission to the one without a practical submission to the other.

In the symbol above the Kingly Crown and the Open Bible represent the inseparable truths of Christ's Kingly and Biblical authority. The Crown and Bible graphics are supplemented by three Bible verses (Ecclesiastes 8:4, Matthew 28:18-20, and Luke 6:46) that reiterate and reinforce the inextricable connection between the authority of Christ as King and the authority of His Word. The truths symbolized by these components are further emphasized by the Latin quotation - *quod scriptura, non iubet vetat*— i.e., "What is not commanded in scripture, is forbidden:' This Latin quote has been considered historically as a summary statement of the regulative principle of Scripture. Together these various symbolic components converge to exhibit the two most foundational Baptist Distinctives out of which all the other Baptist Distinctives arise. Consequently, we have chosen this composite symbol as a logo to represent the primary truths set forth in the *Baptist Distinctives Series.*

PEDOBAPTISM:

IS IT FROM HEAVEN OR OF MEN?

JAMES MARION FROST
1848-1916

PEDOBAPTISM:

IS IT FROM HEAVEN OR OF MEN?

BY

JAMES MARION FROST

With a Biographical Sketch of the Author by John Franklin Jones

"Whether it be right in the sight of God to hearken unto you more than unto God, judge ye." — Acts 4:19

"We ought to obey God rather than men." — Acts 4:29

PHILADELPHIA:
AMERICAN BAPTIST PUBLICATION SOCIETY
1701-1703 CHESTNUT STREET;
1875

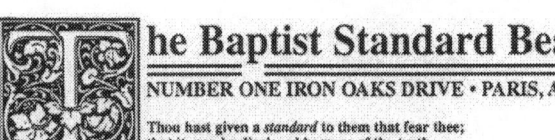

The Baptist Standard Bearer, Inc.
NUMBER ONE IRON OAKS DRIVE • PARIS, ARKANSAS 72855
Thou hast given a *standard* to them that fear thee;
that it may be displayed because of the truth.
-- *Psalm 60:4*

Reprinted 2006

by

THE BAPTIST STANDARD BEARER, INC.
No. 1 Iron Oaks Drive
Paris, Arkansas 72855
(479) 963-3831

THE WALDENSIAN EMBLEM
lux lucet in tenebris
"The Light Shineth in the Darkness"

ISBN# 157978450X

To My Beloved Parents,

Who have cared for me so tenderly, who have watched over me so anxiously, and who have prayed for me so fervently, this little volume is most affectionately inscribed, as a feeble testimonial of the gratitude and the love of their son,

JAMES MARION FROST.

Prefatory Note.

INSTEAD of a formal preface, simply a few words will be offered by way of explanation. When this work was begun, nothing could have been further from the author's expectations and intentions than to write a book. His only purpose was to give the subject a thorough investigation for himself. As it opened up before him, however, and as his interest increased, he determined, in the midst of the investigations, to give the result of his labors to the public, selecting the *Western Recorder* as the medium. The following chapters were, therefore, originally designed as so many articles of a serial for that paper. This fact will account for the marked personal cast they sometimes assume in the way of appeal. Their publication in book-form was first suggested by one of Kentucky's oldest and most judicious pastors, to whom the entire manuscript was read, and whose judgment and opinion deserved the utmost confidence and respect. The advice to put the matter into a small book was taken, partly because it had become rather bulky for a newspaper publication, but especially because it was hoped that by giving to it a more permanent form, more good would eventually be accomplished, which was the sole reason for publishing at all.

It would, perhaps, be well to state also that scattered along through the work, in every chapter, and especially in Chapters IV., VI. and X., are to be found a large number of concessions from Pedobaptist authors. Many of these are new, and all of them very valuable, and if widely circulated will be for the furtherance of gospel truth. Special mention might be made of those quotations, taken from the recent controversy on this subject, published in the *Southern* (Methodist) *Review*, and conducted by two Methodist divines—Rev. A. T. Bledsoe, editor of the *Review*, and one of his brethren, of considerable *notoriety* in this State. These will be of great value to any one studying the subject. Great care has been exercised to preserve perfect accuracy in all the quotations given. All of them, unless otherwise designated, were copied directly from the original works; and those from a second-hand source are taken from the most reliable authorities, whose names are also given. Some Baptist authors have been quoted without mentioning their names.

The quotations are made very accessible by a completed index of authors quoted, arranged in alphabetic order.

The earnest and prayerful endeavor throughout has been to give the subject a purely practical turn. It has been written in a Christian spirit and for a Christian purpose, and is offered for the kindly consideration of those who differ from the positions taken. First read, and then approve or condemn. As the work was designed especially for the masses, any assistance in giving it a wide circulation among them, will be very gratefully received. Already much pleasure, and profit, and real Christian joy have been found in the preparation of the work; and now that it may find its way into the homes and hearts of many, and that, under the gracious influence of the Holy Spirit, the cause of truth may be advanced, while that of error is checked, at least a little, by the contribution of his mite, is the earnest prayer of

THE AUTHOR.

JULY 17, 1875.

Contents.

CHAPTER.		PAGE.
I.	The Scriptures Examined from John's Baptism to the Commission,	9
II.	The Commission—Infants—not in "all nations"—Excluded by Command to Baptize Believers,	22
III.	Infants Excluded from the Commission by what it Further Enjoins,	32
IV.	The Commission the only Authority to Baptize, yet does not Include Infants, as Decided by Pedobaptists. The Acts of the Apostles as far as the Baptism of the Jailer's Household,	51
V.	The Examination of the New Testament Completed,	67
VI.	Infant Communion and Pedobaptists' Concessions,	83
VII.	"Church Identity,"	99
VIII.	Is Baptism in the Room of Circumcision?	114
IX.	The Testimony of History,	136
X.	Six Charges Against the Dogma of Pedobaptism,	154
XI.	Conclusion,	186

Authors Quoted.

	PAGE.
Advocate, The Christian	188
Augustine	149
Barclay	90
Barnes, Dr. Albert	19, 62, 78
Baird, Dr.	195
Baker, Dr. Samuel	147
Basil	147
Bates, Rev. Wm.	183
Baxter, Richard	37
Beecher, Rev. H. W.	118
Bledsoe, Rev. A. T.	
24, 26, 53, 56, 92, 94, 95, 141, 150, 151, 152, 164, 165	
Bloomfield	66
Broadus, Dr. John A.	147
Bunsen	139
Bushnell	114
Calvin, John	54, 163
Campbell, Alexander	172
Campbell, Dr. George	32, 36
Carlstadt and Luther	96
Carson, Alexander	80
Chalmers, Dr.	195
Clarke, Dr. Adam	86
Council of Carthage	150
Coleridge	74, 80
Curcellaeus	139
De Pressensé	134, 152
De Witte, Dr.	70
Dick, Dr. John	54
Field, Dr.	90
Fuller, Bishop	21
Grotius	36
Hahn	138
Hall, Dr. John	197
Hanna, Dr. (in North British Review)	79, 90

AUTHORS QUOTED.

	PAGE.
Hanna, Dr. (in Life of Christ)	91, 114
Herald, The Religious	140, 189
Hibbard, Dr.	29
Hodge, Dr. Charles	134, 151
Hovey, Dr. Alvah	10
Hyppolytus	139
Jacobi, Professor	74, 79, 165
Knapp, Dr.	165
Lange, Professor	98
Liddell and Scott	35
Limborch	89
Luther	139
Mather, Cotton	82
Miller, C. W.	96, 166
Miller, Dr. Samuel	101, 148
Mosheim, Dr.	140, 169
Motley,	174
Müller, Julius	80
Neander, Dr.	48, 74, 89, 139, 163
Olshausen, Dr.	20, 48, 70, 71, 78, 152
Pendleton, Dr. J. M.	29, 31, 102, 134
Pickering's Lexicon	35
Rice, Dr. N. L.	100, 102, 126, 146, 148
Robinson's Lexicon	35, 42
Ryle, Rev. J. C.	54
Salmasius	139, 150
Scott, Dr.	20, 43
Smith, Bishop	197
Sophocles' Lexicon	36
Strarck	162
Stuart, Moses	43, 89, 118, 129, 135
Taylor, Jeremy	162
Turrettine	120
Wall	25, 90, 150
Waller, Rev. J. L.	51, 88
Wesley, Rev. John	183
Whitby, Dr.	62
Wood, Dr.	89, 163
Ypeij and Dermont	70

PEDOBAPTISM:

Is it from Heaven or of Men?

CHAPTER I.

It is simply impossible to overestimate, or to state in exaggerated terms, the importance of doing *just* what our Master has commanded. To study the Scriptures, wherein is recorded his will, is, therefore, a laudable undertaking. These should be studied, not to support a preconceived theory, but that by prayer, earnest, fervent, and by patient labor, the truth may be reached and the Master's will known. To the Bible all theories, confessions, and creeds should be made to bend. In this spirit —our motto being "the Bible, and the Bible alone, is the religion of Protestants"—let the question asked be put to the test. It is no time now for harsh words or unpleasant epithets, much less for sophistry. The inquiry now is what has our Savior commanded? To do that when known, *and only that*, whatever be the consequences, whether persecutions by fines, by stripes, by imprisonment or by death, is honorable indeed, and brings with it the approbation and the blessing of the Master.

The followers of Christ have suffered martyrdom, not more for doing what he commands than for refusing to do what he did not command, and what they regarded as an encroachment upon his ordinance. Did Christ command the baptism of "believers and *their infant children?*" Answer, and act accordingly in the fear of God. Loyalty to Christ is the first thing.

While here and there you find a few bold men who are advancing some new theories of infant baptism, yet the old and oft-repeated arguments in its favor are still being repeated again and again, and are emphasized with fresh vigor all over this land. And to many they are from various causes perfectly conclusive. The following, from Dr. Alvah Hovey, in the *Baptist Quarterly* (for April, 1875, p. 137), is a brief but correct summary of the arguments:

"Baptism is still said to have taken the place of circumcision, the *seal* of the Abrahamic covenant being changed, but not the covenant itself. The Christian Church is still said to be a continuation of the Jewish Church, modeled after it in the quality of its members, part of them being introduced as believers and part of them as unbelievers. The households that were baptized by Paul are still supposed to have included infants who received the holy rite with their believing parents, for may not every household have an infant in it? The language of Christ in blessing little children is still believed to authorize the baptism of infants, for is not any one whom Christ blesses entitled to baptism? The words of Paul in respect to the children of the Corinthian Christians 'but now are they holy' are still supposed to prove that those children were infant members of the Church in Corinth, though the supposition makes the reasoning of Paul wholly illogical. The practice of infant baptism in the third century is still thought to imply its apostolic character, though the practice of immersion at that time, as the only complete rite, is thought to be a perversion, superstitious, if not immodest (Coleman). And the natural desire of Christian parents to have their children in covenant with God is still supposed to justify, in some manner the application of baptism to them, though it is difficult to see why the same argument would not justify the baptism of all whom Christians long to have saved from endless woe—that is to say, the baptism of all mankind."

The frequency and the zeal with which these arguments are repeated, demand that their refutation, so often made, be made again. With this in mind your candid attention is asked to the following pages.

It is by no means easy to learn even from those by whom the rite is practiced and defended, just what is the purpose of infant baptism, or what is the exact status of baptized children. If they die in infancy are they more likely to be saved than those who die of the same age unbaptized? Do they enjoy a single promise not equally enjoyed by the unbaptized children of believing parents— perhaps their older or younger brothers and sisters? Certainly not. Are infants regenerated, "made children of God and heirs of glory" by their baptism? Some Pedobaptists respond yes, while others, with equal emphasis, respond no, and of course the latter are right. Does their baptism make them members of the church? The contrary answers given to this by Pedobaptists are, they are baptized to bring them into the church, and they are baptized because they are already in the church. It is evident, however, that baptized children (infants) are not treated as church-members. They are not disciplined as other members are; they are not allowed to commune as other members are; they are not permitted to participate in the general privileges of the church as other members are. What possible benefit, therefore, can they reap from their baptism? This is an impertinent question, if *God* has *commanded* the baptism of infants. It is simply our duty to obey. These are minor questions, therefore, and with them we have no concern, except so far as they bear upon the leading inquiry: *Pedobaptism; Is it from Heaven or of Men?* This is the standing question of this little volume. *If from heaven*, then to oppose it, or to disregard it, is to be found fighting against God and taking from the sacred word.

If of men, then to defend it and to administer it, by the authority and into the name of the adorable Trinity, is to sin grievously and to add to what is contained in the Scriptures. The question, therefore, is a serious one, for it is a dangerous thing to add to or to take from the inspired oracles. (Revelation xxii. 18, 19.)

This question must be settled by the New Testament. For that is the Christian's only law book, and baptism is a New Testament ordinance. Surely by its decision every one should be willing to abide. To the law and the testimony. And may the Holy

Spirit, its Author, guide us into all truth, blessing both writer and reader.

"O Father of Light! hear our feeble cry, and so illuminate our minds by the influence of the Holy Spirit, that, with an eye single to thy glory, we may look above all the paltry interest of sects and times, and plead the cause of truth alone, desiring only the progress of true Christianity among the children of men."

The first baptism mentioned is that of the Harbinger, who, as Christ's forerunner, came preaching the kingdom of God. The record of his baptism is found in three of the evangelists as follows: Matthew iii. 5-9; Mark i. 4, 5; Luke iii. 3, 7, 8. By reading these narratives carefully you will observe the following facts:

1. Crowds flocked to the baptism of John.

2. Descent from Abraham gave no one a pass to the baptismal waters.

3. Of all who were baptized John demanded repentance, nay, more, evidence of their repentance; "Bring forth fruit meet for" (suitable, agreeable to) "repentance."

4. All admitted to baptism were baptized of him "in Jordan confessing their sins." Do not these simple facts, discernible to even the superficial reader, utterly exclude infants from the subjects of John's baptism?

The epitome of John's baptism, given by Paul in Acts xix. 4, only adds strength to strength:

"Then said Paul, John verily baptized with the baptism of repentance saying unto the people, that they should believe on him which should come after him, that is on Christ Jesus."

In addition to demanding of his hearers that they should repent, he also demanded faith in a coming Messiah. Were infants among John's hearers? Did he demand of infants that they should repent and bring forth fruit meet for repentance? Did he demand of infants that they should believe on him that should come, that is, on Christ Jesus? Were infants baptized confessing their sins? To all of these questions you must give a positive no, unless an infant be capable of doing all these things. There were no infants baptized, therefore, by the first Baptist.

In John iii. 22; iv. 1, 2, is all we have recorded of the baptizing done by Christ and his disciples during his ministry. What his disciples did in his name was said to be done by him. The only point in this, that is pertinent here, is, "that Jesus *made* and baptized more disciples than John." Individuals were first *made disciples*, and then received baptism. There is a manifest difference between *making* disciples and *baptizing* them. As infants could not be made disciples they did not receive baptism. Why give to an infant the badge of discipleship, when it has not been made a disciple? This record, like the other, is not only silent about but utterly excludes infant baptism. The brevity of these narratives is only equaled by the explicitness of their statement of the subjects admitted to the ordinance of baptism in the days of John the Baptist, and the ministry of Christ.

One other passage deserves attention here, and simply because some—only a very few—Pedobaptist consider it as supporting the dogma of infant baptism.

No one would ever think of pausing here, except hailed by a Pedobaptist. And stopping, we find, as will be presently seen, that they are disputing over this passage, as they are in fact over every passage ever quoted in favor of the practice; some claiming, while many more discard it, as supporting the infant rite.

Reference is had to Matthew xix. 13-15, with its parallel passages in Mark x. 13-16, and Luke xviii. 15-17. It requires no close study of the passage to show that the argument founded upon it is baseless. In fact it is refuted by simply a careful reading of the words:

"Then were brought unto him little children, that he should put his hands upon them, and pray; and his disciples rebuked them. But Jesus said, Suffer little children, and forbid them not, to come unto me : for of such is the kingdom of heaven. And he laid his hands on them, and departed thence."

What are the facts? Plainly these, and beyond them no one can go:

1. According to a well-known custom among the Jews, of bringing their children to receive a blessing from distinguished rabbis, children were brought to Jesus also, for this specific purpose, viz: "that he might lay his hands on them, and pray," or bless them. Who will add, and for the purpose of baptizing them? The inspired record does not; and human additions are worthless and dangerous.

2. The disciples rebuked those who brought them. This conduct is unaccountable, if Christ had

hitherto been in the habit of baptizing children, or of even receiving them for the purpose mentioned.

This is *prima facie* evidence that up to this time at least, Pedobaptism was a thing unknown among the apostles.

3. Jesus was displeased, and said, suffer them to come. "*He called* them," says Luke, "unto him." Perhaps, at this time, he is going to give an example which his disciples are to follow, and which he had not yet taught them, viz: of baptizing infants. Don't Pedobaptists wish he had?

4. But he did no such thing. He did simply what the children were brought to him for—nothing more if the divine record can be trusted, viz: "he laid his hands on them," or as Mark has it, "he took them up in his arms, put his hands on them and blessed them," according to the custom already mentioned. If it could only be added as a fifth fact, that he baptized them, what rejoicing there would be among those who baptize infants!

But let the impartial reader say whether these children were baptized, or only blessed, by our Savior. There was a specific thing to be done, and this the Savior did—he laid his hands on them, and blessed them. Is there anything in all this to prove the scripturalness of infant baptism?

A presiding elder recently remarked in the hearing of the writer, "Of course these children were not baptized because they were Jewish children, and having been circumcised would not need to be baptized." Of course he knew from *logical inference* (?) that these children were all *little boys*, and had been circumcised!! But are there no cases in the New Testament, where persons received both the rite of circumcision, and the ordinance of baptism? How about Christ and Paul and Timothy, and the three thousand on the day of Pentecost? If a Jewish family should be converted, and apply for membership in a Methodist Church, would they, or would they not, baptize the circumcised members of the family? But more of this in another chapter.

It has been argued from the phrase "of such is the kingdom of heaven," that these children, whom our Savior blessed, were "members of his visible church." And the conclusion is drawn, that being in the church infants have a right to baptism. But it is wholly gratuitous to assume, that by "the kingdom of heaven" is meant the "visible church." For this, proof is most earnestly demanded. It is an erroneous assumption, born of Pedobaptist reasoning, something like the following: Christ says, these children ("of such is") are in something; they can not be in his spirituaul kingdom, and they were not at that time in the kingdom of glory, therefore, it must mean "visible church," and they are in that. It must be *proved* first, that the expression "kingdom of heaven" is ever used by the inspired writers in a single instance, where it must, from *absolute necessity*, mean the "visible church"—a passage must be produced where it *can not* possibly have any other meaning. It must be *proved*, second, that "the kingdom of heaven," in the passages under consideration, must *necessarily* have that meaning; that it can not mean either the kingdom of glory or Christ's spiritual kingdom, but must of *necessity* mean the "visible church." The question is not what a certain passage of Scripture *may* mean, but what *does* it mean. *Prove* that in this passage the expression can not mean *anything* except " visible church," and so far the argument may be of some avail. But this can not be done.

And, furthermore, even granting that this was its meaning, then the phrase "*of such is* the kingdom," by no means *necessitates* the idea that those of whom it was spoken were *in* the kingdom. It can have, it does have, another interpretation. If not, then the argument would prove too much, and would therefore be worthless. If that be the interpretation, then the passage means that the "kingdom of heaven," whether the " visible church," the kingdom of glory, or Christ's spiritual kingdom, is *composed* " of such " persons (of infants and young children) to the exclusion of persons who are older. If the " visible church " is meant, then the " visible church," in its entirety, and completeness, *consists*, or is made up, "of such." How preposterous! Christ by no means said those children, to whom he gave a blessing, were in the kingdom of heaven; this would simply be impossible, if he had reference to either his spiritual kingdom, or the kingdom of glory. And let it be repeated that it has never been proved that "kingdom of heaven" means "visible church;" nor that "of such" means that those children were *in* the kingdom.

This is all that Christ meant, that those born

into his spiritual kingdom, in some respects resembled children. He refers not so much to children as to childhood. Those born of God are like children, not in age, not in physical stature, not in moral character, but simply in the characteristics of childhood—are gentle, affectionate, docile, confiding, etc.

How strikingly and beautifully do the characteristics of childhood resemble those born into Christ's spiritual kingdom, "who are born not of blood, nor of the will of the flesh, nor of the will of man, but of God." (John i. 13.)

Dr. Albert Barnes, who is good authority among Presbyterians, speaking on this passage, says:

"Of such as these—that is, of persons with such *tempers* as these—is the church composed. He (Christ) does not say of *these infants*, but of such as resemble them, or were *like them* in temper, was the kingdom of heaven made up."

This idea is more fully brought out in Mark and Luke:

"Verily, I say unto you, Whosoever shall not receive the kingdom of God *as a little child*, he shall not enter therein."
Also in Matthew xviii. 3: "Except ye be converted, and become *as little children*, ye shall not enter into the kingdom of heaven." "And whoso shall offend one of these *little ones which believe in* me," etc.

Here the resemblance is still presented, and very strongly indeed. The passage has nothing to do with baptism whatever.

Blessed be the name of Jesus that he said, "Suffer little children, and forbid them not, to come unto me." With great joy should parents, by early instruction, bring their children to him. And none are more earnest than the Baptists in proclaiming this joyous message of our Savior. But in all this there is not one word about infant baptism.

Dr. Scott, a Pedobaptist, in commenting on this passage, says: "Christ did not order these infants to be baptized." Of course not; any one can see that. The passage proves absolutely nothing in favor of that practice. Olshausen, a distinguished German Pedobaptist, in his Commentary, says:* "We can not in truth find anywhere a reliable proof-text in favor of infant baptism."

Why did he not turn to this passage? In his commentary on this very place, he says: † "Of that reference to infant baptism which it is so common to seek in this narrative, *there is clearly not the slightest trace to be found.*" Other men of equal celebrity, and Pedobaptists at that, such as Dr. Doddridge, Prof. Jacobi and others, might be mentioned to the same effect. In fact, many of the most learned Pedobaptists are abandoning this passage as offering no support to infant baptism. Are Baptists, then, to be charged with dullness and stupidity, because they also fail to see here an argument for the practice? The argument can not be very clear. Passing this text, next comes the commission, to be discussed hereafter.

The entire ministry of Christ has now been examined; and though the church, together with the ordinances, have been established, or appointed, yet not one word has been said about the baptism

---

*Quoted in Baptist Short Method. Page 91.
†Progress Baptist Principles, by Curtis. Page 95.

of infants, or of their reception into the church; nay, more, the teaching is wholly at variance with the practice. Is it from heaven, or of men? Says Bishop Fuller,* a distinguished Pedobaptist author: "*We do freely confess there is neither express precept nor precedent in the New Testament for the baptizing of infants.*" Do you believe that?

---

*Quoted in Baptist Short Method. Page 89.

CHAPTER II.

"Go ye therefore, and teach all nations, baptizing them in the name of the Father, and of the Son, and of the Holy Spirit: Teaching them to observe all things whatsoever I have commanded you."—Matt. xxviii. 19, 20.

THIS, with its parallels in Mark xvi. 15, 16, and Luke xxiv. 46, 47, is the Great Commission of our Savior to his disciples—the grand *"Magna Charta"* of his church. Through all his teachings he has said not one word about infant baptism, as was seen in the preceding chapter. After his death and resurrection from the dead, just before he ascended to the glory of the Father, he sends his disciples into the world with this commission. By this he authorizes them to preach the gospel, and to baptize. And here is the only place, so far as the record shows, where he gave this authority. In this, therefore, is contained the *whole law* of Christian baptism. *This is the rule.* All that come after are but examples, and are serviceable to us, simply as illustrating and showing how the commission was understood by those who received it directly from the Master. After all, therefore, *here* the question *must be settled.* By the commission infant baptism must stand or fall. Does it authorize the baptism of infants? Did the disciples so understand it? And did they, in accordance with *this commission*, practice infant baptism? These questions strike at the very vitals of our subject, and will therefore be answered at length in this and following chapters.

If authority to baptize infants be found in the commission, it must be either by a specific, positive command, or, at least, by a *plain, unequivocal, "logical inference."* A command you can not find.

And the only possible way to get *any* inference (one that is plain and logical is simply impossible) is to infer that, as nations are to be baptized, and infants are a part of nations, therefore infants are to be baptized. Is this a plain *"logical* inference?" It may, it does, suit some, but not Baptists surely. The following is a similar specimen of logic: "The wicked shall be turned into hell, with *all the nations* that forget God." Therefore, as infants are a part of the *all nations,* they will—according to this logic—be turned into hell. Is this conclusion admissible? Baptists with one breath exclaim, No! What say Pedobaptists? The logic is precisely the same.

"'Are not infants a part of the all nations spoken of in the commission?' Certainly they are; and so are drunkards, and liars, and swearers, and whoremongers, and infidels, and atheists, and idolaters, and every wicked and abominable person, upon the face of the earth; and if the phrase 'all nations' includes infants, so it does the others, and there is just the same warrant for the baptism of one as the other; that is, *no warrant at all."* The same *infer-*

ence that would baptize the babe would also baptize *each and all of these classes.*

There must surely be something wrong in the logic, which *infers infants to perdition, and persons of such character to the ordinance of Christian baptism.* Those who can, may accept it, but Baptists can not. And, in fact, neither can the more learned Pedobaptists. *E. g.*, when Rev. C. W. Miller, a prominent Methodist preacher in Kentucky, published a book, in which he used this logic, claiming by it to have found a command to baptize infants, he was promptly met and responded to by Dr. A. T. Bledsoe, editor of the *Southern* (Methodist) *Review*,* who is a man of master mind, and wields not only a ready, but a mighty pen. The following is a part of his reply in the *Review*,† showing that he will not accept such logic, though it comes from a Methodist, and that, too, in support of a doctrine he believes:

"Take the command, for example, 'Go ye into all the world, and preach the gospel *to every creature.*' (Mark xvi. 16.) Now here 'the class is' every creature. But stocks and stones and dumb brutes are 'a part of the class.' Shall we then, in obedience to Mr. Miller's logic, preach the gospel to stocks and stones and dumb brutes? Reason and common sense forbid. These compel us, in spite of his logic, to limit the preaching of the gospel, first to human beings, and then to that portion of the class, thus limited, who are capable of hearing and understanding the gospel."

After giving several other examples on the same page, he continues:

---

*This *Review* will be frequently quoted hereafter. It is published in St. Louis, under the auspices of the M. E. Church South. But the editor, one of the brightest lights in that church, resides in Baltimore, Md. †For July 1874, p. 176.

"Not to multiply similar instances, as we might do *ad infinitum*, we conclude with this one: 'The Lord said unto Joshua, Make thee sharp knives, and circumcise again *the children of Israel* the second time. (Joshua v. 2.) Here the 'class is' the children of Israel. But yet, instead of applying this command to 'all the children of Israel,' every reader of the Bible limits it to *male* children, in conformity with the well-known custom of the Jews."

So the " all nations" in the commission must be limited to those who have been made disciples, who, having heard the gospel, *have believed* on the Savior which it offered.

Pedobaptists must show, here, either a *positive, specific* command to baptize infants, or, at least, a plain, "*logical inference*," which will support the practice, and yet be in perfect keeping with the entire teaching of God's word. It is just to demand this; and, until they comply, they are chargeable with "teaching for doctrine the commandments of men." Baptists are not, as is sometimes charged, afraid of *inferences*. They will accept such an one as is here demanded—but no other—whenever it is produced.

But, indeed, Dr. Wall and many other eminent Pedobaptists cordially admit that the commission does not ordain infant baptism. When they surrender the commission, all is surrendered. (See Chapter IV.) Dr. Wall, in the preface to his "History of Infant Baptism" (page 29), as quoted by John L. Waller,* says, in this commission, "that there is no particular direction given what they were to do in reference to the children of those

---

*In *Western Baptist Review*, Vol. I. p. 162.

that received faith, and among all those persons that are recorded as baptized by the apostle, there is no express mention of any infants." And, turning from the New Testament as insufficient to establish who are the subjects of a New Testament ordinance, he builds his argument for infant baptism on Jewish-proselyte baptism. Surely that is a sandy foundation, for many of the ablest *Pedobaptist writers*, the world has ever known, have denied most emphatically, that there was any such thing as Jewish-proselyte baptism.

And Dr. Bledsoe, showing that nothing is found in the commission in favor of the rite, says: "In fact, one of the very best works ever written in favor of infant baptism—namely, the work of Dr. Samuel Miller, of Princeton, *does not draw a single argument* from Matthew xxviii. 19"*—that is, from the commission. From these facts, is it not perfectly evident that the commission does not authorize the practice? That so far as the commission is concerned, Pedobaptism is not from heaven? *And yet this is our only authority to baptize?* Bear that in mind. But, furthermore, the commission, given by our Savior as the law of Christian baptism, not only does not authorize the baptism of infants, but absolutely excludes them as subjects of that ordinance.

IN COMMANDING THE BAPTISM OF BELIEVERS, THE COMMISSION EXCLUDES THE BAPTISM OF ALL OTHER CLASSES— WHETHER IDIOTS, UNBELIEVERS OR INFANTS.

---

*Southern Review, for July, 1874, 177.

That the Savior does, here, command to baptize believers, no one will for a moment call in question, unless perchance he has a purpose to serve. It is universally admitted that a believer in the Lord Jesus Christ is a scriptural subject for Christian baptism. In Mark's version of this same commission, it is said, "he that BELIEVETH and is baptized," etc., evidently connecting faith with, and giving it a priority to baptism. From these parting words of the Master, both Baptists and Pedobaptists get their authority for the practice of believer's baptism. *That it is specified in this commission will not, therefore, be denied.*

And this very specification excludes, forever, the baptism of infants. But you say, "Christ did not forbid it." Was it necessary for Christ to command, thou shalt not baptize unbelievers—infidels, or atheists, or liars, or adulterers, etc.? thou shalt not baptize idiots; thou shalt not baptize houses; thou shalt not baptize dumb brutes; thou shalt not baptize bells; thou shalt not baptize infants, and so on through the whole range of created things? Most assuredly not. It was only necessary for him to *specify* or *mention* one class, which he did in commanding *believers* to be baptized. And by that specification all other classes, infants just as effectually as the rest, are excluded. By the command, *baptize believers*, infant baptism is as really forbidden as was any one of the classes named above. This is in accordance with a very common law maxim taken from Blackstone, and in every-day use, viz: "*The expression of one thing is the ex-*

clusion of another." The correctness of this principle will not be called in question by any one. Many examples illustrating it, both in and out of the Bible, will at once occur to the thoughtful reader. One will be given, viz: the command to offer the paschal lamb. (See Exodus xii.) There was no need of God saying to Moses, you must not take a heifer; you must not take a lamb that has blemish, or one that is two or three years old; you must not get a female; you must not put the blood inside the house, etc. But when he commanded, take a lamb—of the first year—a male—without blemish, that the blood be put on the two side-posts, and on the upper door-posts, etc.—*every thing* else was excluded, except just what he had specified in his command—as much so as if he had forbidden each one of the particulars by name.

Now apply this principle, universally recognized as true, to the commission, where we have *believer's baptism mentioned, specifically* and *positively commanded.* What, then, becomes of all other baptisms? The conclusion is irresistible—they are excluded—that of infants with the rest.

Did Christ, by his command to baptize those that believe in him, forbid the baptism of all unbelievers, of idiots, and of base, immoral persons, of stocks or stones, of houses or bells? Then did he also just as effectually, and as truly, forbid also the baptism of infants. It is, therefore, excluded from the commission. By what law? By the law of Him who "is over all, God blessed forever." There is no rack of interpretation, by which a law to baptize believers, can be tortured to include the baptism of the unconscious babe. Even Dr. Hibbard, who has been called the Carson of Methodism, in his "Christian Baptism," p. 236, admits, as quoted by Dr. Pendleton,* that "a command to baptize *believers* is no authority for baptizing *infants*." Certainly, then, the commission is " no authority for baptizing infants," for it is " a command to baptize believers." Such is the decision even of this distinguished Pedobaptist.

"It may be more satisfactory to present the argument in syllogistic form. Here it is: 'A command to baptize *believers* is no authority for baptizing *infants*.' The commission contains a command to baptize believers; therefore, the commission is no authority for baptizing infants."† These premises are admitted, and you can not reject the conclusion. Then " the commission of Christ to the apostles in requiring them to baptize disciples, believers, prohibits in effect the baptism of all others. It will not do to say we are not forbidden in so many words to baptize infants. The same may be said of unbelievers; aye, of houses, and cattle, and bells."

You ask, however, " could not Christ have given another commission which would have authorized the baptism of infants?" Certainly he could. But did he do it? The fact, that infants are excluded from this commission, does not preclude his giving another. But who has ever found that other com-

---

*" Three Reasons," p. 15. †Same, p. 16.

mission, wherein infant baptism is commanded? In what chapter and verse of the New Testament do *you* find it? What rejoicing there would be if Pedobaptists could point their finger to one single chapter or verse in all the New Testament, and say, here it is, a plain command to baptize "believers and their infant children." The very welkin would be made to ring with the outbursts of their joy, as they would exclaim "*Eureka! Eureka!*" And no one could blame them. But there is no such place, nor one that even hints at any such thing. (See Chapter VI.) Here, and here alone, is the authority to baptize, and by this commission no authority is given to baptize the unconscious babe.

And, furthermore, if a command were found in the Bible to baptize infants, *that* would not do away with *this* commission. *It* would still require that they, even those baptized in infancy, be baptized when they become believers in the Lord Jesus. Or, as the great Carson puts it:

"This commission, to baptize believers, does not indeed imply that it is impossible that another commission might have been given to baptize infants, but, by necessity, it excludes them forever from being included in this command. If infants are baptized, it is from another commission; and it is another baptism founded on another principle. But not only does this commission exclude infants from the baptism it enjoins; if there were even another commission enjoining the baptism of infants, when these infants, who have been baptized in infancy according to this supposed second commission, believe the gospel. they must be baptized according to this commission (Matthew xxviii. 19), without any regard to their baptism in infancy. The commission commands all men to be baptized on believing the gospel."*

To the candid it must be evident that this baptism, by its very command, is limited to believers, those who are made disciples. And this will be corroborated by a further examination of the commission, in the following chapter.

Unconscious infants can not believe, and, therefore, from necessity they are excluded from baptism. This chapter will be closed by the following quotation from Dr. J. M. Pendleton:†

"I know it will be said, for it has been said a thousand times, that if infants are not to be baptized because they can not believe, they can not be saved because they can not believe. If the salvation of infants depends on their faith, they can not be saved. They are incapable of faith. They are doubtless saved through the mediation of Christ, but it is not by faith. It seems to me that our opponents egregiously fail to accomplish their object in urging this objection to our view. They must intend to make us admit the propriety of infant baptism, or force us to a denial of infant salvation. We make neither the admission nor the denial. As soon as we say that infants are not saved by faith, but without faith, their objection is demolished."

---

*His Work on Baptism, p. 170. †"Three Reasons," p. 19.

CHAPTER III.

INFANTS ARE UTTERLY INCAPABLE OF BEING THE SUBJECTS OF A SINGLE ONE OF THE THREE THINGS WHICH THE COMMISSION ENJOINS, and of course, therefore, they are necessarily excluded from it, and from the baptism it enjoins. Read carefully again the words of the Master as given in Matthew xxviii. 19, 20; Mark xvi. 16, and Luke xxiv. 46, 47. These are the different versions of the *great commission* given by our Savior to his disciples.

What is enjoined in this commission? The answer is found in the language of Dr. George Campbell, a distinguished Presbyterian of Scotland. In his notes on this passage, he says:

"There are manifestly three things which our Lord here distinctly enjoins his apostles to execute with regard to the nations, *to-wit: Matheteuine, baptizine, didaskine*; that is, to CONVERT *them to the faith, to initiate the converts* into the church by baptism, and to *instruct the baptized* in all the duties of the Christian life."

Noticing the emphasized words, would any one suppose, that either of the things enjoined could have for its subject an unconscious infant? Could an unintelligent babe be *converted to the faith?* Or could it be among the *converts* "initiated" into the church by baptism? Or could it be among the *baptized converts* who were to be *instructed* in all the duties of the Christian life? Please pardon the asking of such simple questions, for the theory here opposed makes it necessary to ask them. It is proposed to take each injunction of the commission separately, and to ask if that can be executed with regard to an infant.

The Savior commands that the disciples go, *and first*, "TEACH ALL NATIONS," or as Mark gives it, "Preach the gospel to every creature." The word "teach," it will be observed, is used twice in Matthew's version of the commission. In the original, two words are used, and evidently mean different things. The question now before us is simply this, What is meant by the word "*teach*," as first used, which is a translation of the Greek word (*matheteuo*)?

By the advocates of Pedobaptism, *i. e.*, some of them, it has been argued that the word (*matheteuo*, here rendered teach) means simply to enroll as scholars, as a parent would assign his children to a school, and that, therefore, it does not mean to teach, and may in that sense be applied to infants as well as to adults.

But the simple fact that the word in the King James translation is rendered *teach* is very strong presumptive evidence that it involves the idea of *instruction*. That the word, although its full meaning is not expressed by the English word *teach*, does involve the idea of instruction; that it means to *make disciples by instruction, i. e., by preaching the gospel, is most unquestionably true, and is sustained by the very best authority among*

Pedobaptist scholars. In fact, this is denied only by those who have felt that their cause was in a desperate condition. That such is the meaning of the word will appear, however, from the following considerations:

1. The word (*matheteuo*) is used only four times in the New Testament, and in each of the other three places, is *limited necessarily to adults, and necessiates the idea of instruction.*

"Every scribe who is *instructed* (*matheteutheis*) unto the kingdom of heaven, is like unto a man that is a householder, which bringeth forth out of his treasure things new and old." (Matthew xiii. 52.) "A rich man of Arimathea, named Joseph, who also himself was Jesus' *disciple (ematheteuse).*" (Matthew xxvii. 57.) "And when they had preached the gospel to that city, and had *taught* (*matheteusantes*) many," etc. (Acts xiv. 21.)

Paul and Barnabas, acting under this very command of Jesus, preached the gospel to the people of Derbe, and by their preaching many were *made disciples*. In these three instances the force of the verb (*matheteuine*) can not be mistaken. No one will deny, that in these cases it refers to adults alone, and, at least, *involves* the idea of instruction. And it is scarcely possible that the word would be used in a different sense in the only remaining place, where it is found in the New Testament, and that, too, as it is used by Matthew, the same author, who makes use of it in *two* of the other places.

2. The word here used by our Savior is a *derivative* word, which being traced to its origin gives the same meaning. It comes from a noun (*math-*

etes), which all through the New Testament is translated *disciple*. This is its uniform meaning and translation. And notwithstanding this noun disciple (*mathetes*) is found in the New Testament about *two hundred and sixty-four times,* yet *not even once* is it so used as that unintelligent infants could be included.

This is significant in its bearing upon our subject; but not at all singular. For this noun itself is derived from another Greek verb (*manthano*), which is always used in the sense of learning, and of being taught or instructed ; and is defined by Pickering, in his Greek Lexicon, as follows : " *To learn, understand, to seek to learn* or *inquire about,*" etc. It seems to carry the idea of imparting instruction where inquiry is made. It is well to keep before our minds that from whatever side the word (*matheteuo*) in the commission is approached, infants are by its very meaning excluded, as incapable of being its subjects.

3. As lexicons are based upon the use of words, depending upon that for their definitions, of course this word will be defined by them in harmony with its use as pointed out above. Hence, we have the following definitions, from the very best authorities, given to this word (*matheteuo*).

Pickering—" *To teach, to be a scholar.*"

Liddell and Scott—" *To make a disciple of* any one, N. T.: pass. *To be instructed.*"

Robinson's Lexicon of N. T. Greek—"*To disciple. To train as a disciple, to teach, to instruct.*"

Sophocles.—"*To be a mathetes.*" "2. *To make a disciple of, to instruct.*"

This authority and these definitions will not be questioned by any one capable of judging.

4. With such testimony before you, as to the meaning of the word, you can not miss the meaning of our Savior when he gave this command, " Go *teach* all nations." Nor are you surprised when it is said: The almost unanimous rendering of these words by commentators and translators is, "*make disciples* of [from among] all nations," which was to be done by such instruction as was imparted in preaching the gospel. Adam Clarke, on this, says: " *Make disciples of all nations, bring them to an acquaintance with God who bought them, and then baptize them,*" etc. " *It is natural,*" he adds, in view of this fact, " *to suppose that adults were the first subjects of baptism.*"

Grotius, a learned German commentator, as quoted by Mr. Alexander Campbell,* says: *Matheteuo* "means *to communicate the first or elementary principles, and then after baptiziny those who receive these rudimental views*, teach (*didasko*) or introduce them as persons initiated into the higher branches of Christian doctrine."

Dr. George Campbell, in his translation of the New Testament, renders this by "*convert the nations.*" And then in his notes on it says: " Wynne in saying '*make disciples,*' has hit exactly the sense of *matheteuo.*" And further says that here he

---
*Lex. Debate, p. 367.

(Campbell) has used the word "*convert*" in the same sense. This translation *necessitates* in the word the ideas both of *instruction* and *persuasion*—the only means by which persons could be *converted*.

Other Pedobaptist authority might be given, but let these suffice.

This construction of the text agrees with the language of Mark: "*Preach the gospel* to every creature;" and of Luke, "that *repentance and remission of sins should be preached* in his name among all nations."

Surely Richard Baxter,* one of the most pious Pedobaptists that ever lived, had the spirit as well as the meaning of these men when he wrote the following interpretation of this passage:

"By the first teaching or *making disciples, that must go before baptism,* is meant the convincing of the world that Jesus is the Christ, the true Messiah, anointed of God with fullness of grace, and of the Spirit without measure, and sent to be the Savior and Redeemer of the world; *and when they were brought to acknowledge this, then they were to baptize them,*" etc.

He also says:

"*Matheteuo* means to preach the gospel to all nations, and *to engage them to believe it, in order to their profession of that faith by baptism.*"

Such is the meaning of the word as defined by even Pedobaptists themselves. Now, is it possible to apply this word to an infant? Is it possible for an unintelligent babe to be the subject of what is expressed in the word *metheteuo* (here rendered

---
*Campbell and Rice Lex. Debate, p. 381.

teach)—to be *instructed, persuaded, brought to an acquaintance with God, to be made a disciple by the preaching of the gospel?* Most assuredly not. From the very meaning of the word, as understood by Pedobaptists, infants can not be *made disciples.* And, as we have seen, the word (disciple) is nowhere used so as to include the infant; but, rather, the word (*mathetes*) of which it is a translation entirely precludes any such idea—*a babe be a learner,* or a *babe be a disciple,* how monstrously absurd! " If any man [man is supplied, *any one*] will come after me [will be my disciple], let him deny himself, and take up his cross, and follow me." (Matthew xvi. 24.) "And whosoever doth not bear his cross, and come after me, can not be my disciple." (Luke xiv. 27.) Can an infant deny itself? Can it take up, and bear its cross? Can it follow Christ? You must answer *no. Then it can not be Christ's disciple.* It is to no purpose to urge that they were made disciples by baptizing them. How trivial this often repeated objection appears in view of what has been already written! And, further, if infants are *made disciples* by baptism, so are adults. Is it possible, that by baptism an individual is made a *believer* or a *disciple,* when he must be *that* before he receives the ordinance? And "if persons are made *believers* or *disciples* by baptizing, why require faith of adults in order to their admission to the ordinance, seeing they would receive faith by being baptized? And let us carry out this doctrine; and since the thing may be done, let us look at the result of its operation. An infidel, by being baptized, becomes a believer in Jesus! Idolaters and Jews, as was done by order of some of the Roman emperors and of Charlemagne, being taken by force and baptized, become disciples! Those infants in Germany who, not long since, were torn from the arms of their Baptist parents, and baptized by order of the civil magistrates, were made disciples of Christ! The untold millions of the unconverted [some of them the basest of the baser sort], now living and that have lived, who were baptized in infancy, were all made, by their baptism, disciples or believers!! And a Turk, a worshiper of Juggernaut, or of Boodh, would become a disciple by simply baptizing him!" If an infant is a disciple, it is an *untaught, unbelieving disciple!!*

What a solecism! " Oh the follies of infant baptism! Your name is legion!"

Paul rejoiced in *making disciples,* but was thankful that so few were *baptized* by him at Corinth. He was sent to the Gentiles, commissioned "to open their eyes, and to turn them from darkness to light, and from the power of Satan unto God, that they may receive forgiveness of sins, and inheritance among them which are sanctified by faith that is in me." (Acts xxvi. 18.) Paul was sent to *make disciples,* not by baptizing, but by preaching the gospel of the grace of God, which he preached so fervently and in which he always rejoiced. He distinctly declares: "Christ sent me not to baptize, but to preach the gospel." (1 Corinthians i. 17.) To preach the gospel and to *make disciples* was one thing, while to baptize them was altogether another thing, in the sight of this grand old apostle. He but imitated his Master who *made and baptized* disciples—*first* making men disciples, and *then* giving them the badge of discipleship. Baptists have ever been satisfied to follow in the wake of their Master and his immediate and inspired apostles; and, therefore, they have never practiced the baptizing of unconscious infants. Baptists, by preaching the gospel, make disciples, and then baptize them.

Again, the *second* injunction of the commission is *to administer the ordinance of Christian baptism*. "*Baptizing them into the name*," etc.

"Baptizing them."—Whom? Evidently those previously made disciples.

If all the nations were *made disciples*, or became believers in the Lord Jesus, then all the nations were to be baptized. But if not, then only *that part of the nation* were to be baptized, who were made disciples by the preaching of the gospel. It has been shown above that the "all nations" must be understood in a limited sense, or we are forced to conclusions so absurd that no one will accept them. So far as the grammatical construction of the sentence is concerned,* the relative pronoun "*them*" (*autous*, although of the masculine gender), may have for its antecedent either the "*all nations*" (*ethna*, which is neuter gender), or the noun *disciples*, which, although not expressed in the preceding clause, yet is supposed and understood in the verb

---

* Winer's Greek Grammar of N. T., pp. 141, 146.

(*matheteusate*) " teach," *or make disciples*. Whichever be the case, Christ himself has most certainly, by the verb *teach*, or make disciples, limited the "*all nations,*" so far as it contains the parties to be baptized, and is referred to by the pronoun "*them.*" And the true sense seems, then, to be, that it (the pronoun) looks to the " all nations" as its antecedent—*but to the " all nations" as limited by Christ with the verb " teach."*

In pointing out the subjects for baptism, the pronoun ("*them*") refers, therefore, no more to infants, who are, indeed, a part of the "all nations," *but who can not be made disciples*, than to drunkards and liars, infidels and atheists, or idiots even; all of whom are a part of the " all nations," but who have not been made disciples of the Lord Jesus Christ—that is, are not believers, rejoicing in the hope of the glory of God. Again, therefore, we are shut up to believer's baptism; while infants are excluded by necessity.

But furthermore, *infants are utterly incapable of receiving the ordinance of Christian baptism.* It is not meant that infants can not be immersed as was formerly done, or sprinkled as is now done by Pedobaptists; but that an infant can not be baptized, as Christ commanded that ordinance to be administered. This commission is our only authority for baptizing any one; and consequently this is our only baptismal formula. And instead of its authorizing the baptism of infants, it rather excludes them from that ordinance.

"*Baptizing them*"—but why stop, that does not finish the command? Read it through, and see if it does not exclude infants. "Baptizing then INTO *the name of the Father, and of the Son, and of the Holy Spirit.*" These words, while they give a command to baptize believers, at the same time cut up infant baptism "root and branch." What is meant by "baptizing *into the name*," etc.? Truly, it signifies that the act is done by the authority of the Triune God. And he who baptizes an infant by this formula—and no other is used—says, by the action, he does it by the *authority of the adorable Trinity*. But Pedobaptists have never shown that authority to the world—if they have ever found it. "Who hath required this at your hands?"

But the expression, "*baptized into the name*," has another signification, and one that is exceedingly suggestive and impressive.

Surely, no one will object if those who defend the practice of Pedobaptism be allowed to tell what that signification is. Their testimony therefore will be given.

Robinson, in his Greek Lexicon, says:

"To be BAPTIZED INTO (*baptizo eis*) a person or the name of a person, is to be baptized into a *profession of faith in and sincere obedience to the person.*"

Baptism by this formula, therefore, is a *profession of faith in and a pledge of sincere obedience* to the Trinity. But an infant has no faith; can make no profession; can not pledge obedience.

Moses Stuart, as quoted by the *Western Baptist Review*,* says:

"The word baptize may be followed by a person or a thing (doctrine) which has *eis* before it. In the first case, when it is followed by a person, it means by the sacred rite of baptism, *to bind one's self to be a disciple or follower of a person, to receive or obey his laws* * * * *or it means to acknowledge him as Sovereign. Lord, and Sanctifier.* E. g., Matthew xxviii. 19," *i. e.*, the commission.

Can one word of all this be applied to an unintelligent babe? When baptized *into the name*, does the infant express any profession of faith? Does it bind *itself* to be a disciple or a follower? Does it, thereby, *obligate* ITSELF *to obey the doctrines and the laws of Christ?* Does it acknowledge the Trinity, claiming the Father as its Sovereign, the Son as its Lord, the Holy Spirit as its Sanctifier?

To ask these questions of an intelligent person, is to answer them in the negative. And yet the infant must do this in being admitted to the ordinance of Christian baptism! With this formula *infants* are baptized! Could any thing be more supremely absurd?

In his commentary on this passage, Dr. Scott, another Pedobaptist, says:

"To be baptized, therefore, '*into the name* of the Father, and of the Son, and of the Holy Ghost,' *implies a professed dependence* on these three *divine Persons, jointly and equally, and a devoting of* OURSELVES *to them as worshipers and servants.*"

---
* Vol. I. p. 243.

Every word of this is true. But it is absolutely without any meaning in the baptism of infants. It is worthy of notice that these distinguished advocates for infant baptism have not even left room for the *sponsors*. But they tell us truly, that it signifies an act done for "*one's self*" and a "*devoting of ourselves*" to the worship and service of the Trinity.

It is unnecessary to tell an intelligent reader, that the words, quoted from Robinson, Stuart and Scott, all of whom are Pedobaptists of high rank, are, whether so intended or not, the ax laid at the root of the tree of Pedobaptism.

Already its boughs are trembling, and sooner or later, beneath the strokes of the glistening steel, it must fall. You may immerse the infant, you may sprinkle water into its upturned face, smiling in beauty before you; but never with the least shadow of meaning can you baptize an unintelligent babe, "*into* the name of the Father, and of the Son, and of the Holy Spirit."

Again, there is another fact which, inasmuch as it shows that the infant can not receive this ordinance, may, with propriety, be mentioned in this connection.

"*Baptism is the answer of a good conscience toward God.*" (1 Peter iii. 21.) The judgments of conscience are based upon a knowledge of actions as right or wrong. Like a just judge, the conscience gives its decisions, according to the knowledge of the case, which is obtained by the facts presented. But as infants can not have a knowledge of their action in baptism, they can not have, therefore, the answers of a good conscience in relation to that act. Baptism can not be to them the "answer of a good conscience," but is a nullity.

The judgments of conscience, moreover, have reference only to a person's own actions. One person can have neither a good nor a bad conscience in relation to the actions of any other person or persons. Baptism, as administered to an infant, with a sponsor, is not its own personal act. The babe knows nothing about it, and therefore can not have the answer of a good conscience in reference to it. As infants, therefore, can not know right and wrong, and can not have the answer of a good conscience in their baptism, neither can they receive Christian baptism, for it is "not the putting away of the filth of the flesh, but the answer of a good conscience toward God." An intelligent, conscientious young lady, well known to the writer, anxious to know if her infant baptism was acceptable obedience to Christ, as is the case of every one who loves Jesus in sincerity and in truth, was referred to this line of argument. After long, earnest and prayerful inquiry, reading and conversation with Christian friends, she reasoned about as follows: "My parents tell me I was baptized in infancy, but as Christian baptism is the answer of a good conscience toward God (1 Peter iii. 21), and as I know nothing about my infant baptism, and as it was not my own act (but the act of my parents), I did not have the answer of a good conscience toward God, and it, therefore, was not Christian baptism. And, hence, I am *unbaptized*, and it is my duty to obey Christ in that ordinance."

What a struggle to tear away from and count as a nullity the baptism (?) given by her parents! But while she loved them, she loved her Savior more. And as a result of that struggle she was soon buried with Christ in baptism, and has ever since rejoiced in the answer of a good conscience toward God. Sometimes it is said in answer to this, that when persons, baptized in infancy, become believers, they adopt their infant baptism, and thus make it their own act. Were this so, even then it follows that they are without baptism, through all those intervening years, until the act is so adopted. And if they can adopt baptism as the act of their parents, and thus make it their own, why not adopt any other act, as the worship and the service of their parents? This would indeed be serving God by proxy! Infant *communion*, having been introduced along with infant baptism about the third century, has long since been abandoned because infants can not discern the Lord's body in that ordinance. So now, infant baptism—its twin-sister—should be abandoned, because infants can not have the answer of a good conscience toward God in this ordinance. But taking a somewhat different view of this passage, the same result is reached. The conscience, having been made good in regeneration, demands that we render obedience to Christ in the act of baptism. And our baptism is the answer or the response given to that demand of a good conscience toward God. No conscience is good, nor will it make this demand, previous to its being purged from dead works, and purified by the blood of Christ.

The conscience of an infant is not purified, and, as the infant has not been regenerated, it is not "*a good* conscience," and, therefore, it makes no demands to which the baptism is an answer.

The conscience of an infant, moreover, because of its own natural weakness, can not make any demands. To what, then, is the baptism of an infant an answer or a response? Echo answers—What? And further, conscience demands that this act of obedience in baptism, as in everything else, shall be a *personal act*. It is sheer folly to talk about the demands of your conscience being answered or satisfied by the acts of some one else! Hence, parents can not act for the child in this matter. Sponsors are unknown in the New Testament, as also in church history for years after the apostles. Obedience by proxy is one of the many absurd inventions of men, necessitated by the exigencies of Pedobaptism. "Every one must give an account of *himself* unto God." That the conscience of those baptized in infancy is satisfied and approves, in later years, the baptism given them by their parents, proves nothing. For what is the approbation, or the satisfaction of a *perverted* conscience? The perverted conscience of Saul of Tarsus approved, while he persecuted the Church of Christ. For he verily thought that in doing so he did God service.

Is it not the part of candor to admit that infants are incapable of being the subjects of the second injunction of the commission—are unable to receive the ordinance of Christian baptism?

The *third* thing enjoined is, *that those previously made disciples and baptized, shall be further taught in all the commands of Christ.* "Teaching them" (*i. e.*, the baptized disciples) "to observe all things whatsoever I have commanded you."

Of course this can not apply to unintelligent infants, as they are incapable of being *taught*. The three injunctions of the commission have all been considered. Christ commanded, make disciples, baptize, and teach. Of these three things, it has been seen, not one, (even baptism) can be executed upon an infant. It was this fact that lead the great German Pedobaptist commentator, Olshausen, after stating in his notes on Lydia's household-baptism (see Chapter V.) that "there is altogether wanting any conclusive proof-text for the baptism of children in the age of the apostles," to add the following foot-note: "In the words describing the *institution* of baptism, in Matthew xxviii. 19, the connection of *matheteuine, discipling*, with *baptizine, baptizing*, and *didaskine, appears quite positively to oppose the idea that the baptism of children entered at first into the view of Christ.*"

Here we have the institution of baptism by *Christ himself*, yet the very things enjoined show, as this Pedobaptist says, that Christ had no reference to the baptizing of infants. And Neander *

---

*Rice and Campbell Debate, p. 895.

also, the Pedobaptist church historian, says: "IT IS CERTAIN THAT CHRIST DID NOT ORDAIN INFANT BAPTISM." How could an honest man, who was a reader of the New Tesament, and a writer of church history, say otherwise? If Christ did not institute it, then it is of men. It might be well to state here that the *order* laid down in the commission—make disciples, baptize, and teach—is the *divine* order, given by Christ. And let no one be so presumptuous as to think that he can improve on the divine plan, and baptize individuals—infants even—previous to their being at least professed disciples.

This is the *natural* order, too. For who, of their own will and choice, will submit to Christ's command, to be baptized, until they become Christ's disciples—until they love him? "If ye love me, keep my commandments," is the test which Christ laid down for all. Obedience, to be acceptable to him, must be willing and personal, and must spring from a heart that *loves*. "And every one that loveth is born of God."* Whenever it is necessary, in order to support a given theory, to transpose the words of Scripture, the correctness of the theory itself may well be suspected. Pedobaptism, to be sustained, demands not only a change in the order of the words in Christ's command, but a perversion of the very words he used in giving that command.

No one will gainsay the soundness, the naturalness and scripturalness of the following paraphrase,

---
*1 John iv. 7.

which is offered only as an interpretation, of the commission:

"Go ye, therefore, and" (no longer confining your labors to the Jews) "make disciples from among *all nations*, baptizing them" (*i. e.*, those whom you have previously made disciples from the nations) "into the name of the Father, and of the Son, and of the Holy Spirit; teaching them" (*i. e.*, those previously made disciples and baptized) "to observe all things whatsoever I have commanded you. And lo, I am with you alway, even to the end of the world." This is the order which our Savior gave. And let no one dare to violate it, even to support a pet theory.

If more than this was commanded, it was not obeyed, for those commissioned certainly did no more. Guided as they were by the Divine Spirit, they did just as they were commanded—no more and no less. Their practice, therefore, will plainly exhibit what they understood by this commission of their Lord and ours.

CHAPTER IV.

BEFORE passing to the practice of the apostles, however, another remark may be made on the commission. True, its discussion has already been rather protracted, but so important is its bearing upon the subject under consideration, that its full force can not be too fully developed or too urgently pressed. For, the whole question is settled by *this commission.* It has been previously stated, and let the remark be reiterated with double emphasis, that *the commission* is the *only authority* we have for administering the ordinance of Christian baptism to *any one; and the subjects of baptism therefore must be limited to those mentioned in this commission.* Mark and Luke do not give another, but simply a different version of the same commission.

Says an able Baptist writer, Rev. John L. Waller:*

"This passage (Matthew xxviii. 19, 20) is all the authority in the Scriptures for the use of the solemn and awful name of the Trinity in baptism; and all who baptize infants use this name in their ministration. The true question is: *Does this commission authorize the baptism of infants?* If it does not, the minister who baptizes an in-

*In *Western Baptist Review*, Vol. I. p. 161.

fant in the name of the Father, and of the Son, and of the Holy Spirit, acts without divine warrant, and performs as much an act of will-worship as if he baptized a bell in this name. But if this commission does warrant infant baptism, then the inference may legitimately be drawn that it was practiced by the apostles and their co-laborers, although no instance of their having done so may be upon record. The commission, then, must settle the controversy."

When Christ gave this command—his only recorded words in reference to the ordinance—he thereby issued, and perpetuated to the end of time, *the whole law of Christian baptism.* And by this his disciples must be controlled until he revokes the order, or gives another that will nullify this one. He certainly gave no other command—so far as the inspired account can be relied upon—while he was here on earth. From Matthew to Revelation it can not be found.

This is conceded—it is even affirmed—by C. W. Miller, one of the most zealous, though not one of the most judicious advocates of Pedobaptism, belonging to the Methodist denomination. If the rite, therefore, be not authorized in this commission, then it can not claim for itself to be of divine appointment, but must rest under the charge of being from man. *Does it get any authority here?* This is the naked question before us.

The candid reader, it is believed, will answer this question in the negative.

However this may be with *you*, it is none the less true, that a decided and emphatic negative is given to this very question by a large number of the most learned advocates of infant baptism. Although making out (?), as they suppose, their cause in some other way, yet, in plain words, and by fair implications, they have asserted over and over again, that this text (Matthew xxviii. 19) has no reference whatever to infant baptism. Pedobaptism has received its death-blow from such concessions, which honest men are compelled to make, despite their belief in the dogma.

From an article published in the *Southern* (Methodist) *Review*,* and written by its able editor, Rev. A. T. Bledsoe, LL.D., a few quotations will here be given. The object of this article was to show that the claim made by C. W. Miller, to have found "a *command* for the baptism of infants," was false—a strange issue, indeed, to be made between two Methodist divines. And you may see how the Doctor carries the fort with a perfect storm. He says:

"Now, no one can, at first sight, see any command for infant baptism in these words (Matthew xxviii. 19); for they contain no mention, whatever, of infants, or of infant baptism."

Again:

"Let him (Mr. Miller) begin at home, and first convince the great lights of Pedobaptism that he has found 'a *command* for infant baptism,' [!! marvelous, indeed; don't they believe *that!!!*] and then we may entertain some better hopes of his success abroad. But, until then, we fear his discovery [of a command to baptize infants], however

---

* For July 1874, pp. 226, 227, 228.

original, will only be laughed at by our adversaries, and his exploits deemed a little quixotical."

Again:

"John Calvin was certainly a great master in logic. Grant his premises and he is a match for the world. Yet his logic, clear and strong as it was, did not enable him to see in Matthew xxviii 19, anything like a command for infant baptism. Nay, he even admitted that those words, in themselves considered, *relate to adults only, and have* no reference to infants. * * * Thus, in spite of all his zeal for infant baptism, he found *no proof for the doctrine* in Matthew xxviii., much less an 'express command' in its favor. * * * He admits, as we have seen, that the words of Matthew xxviii. 19, 20, *relate exclusively* to *adults, and to no others.*"

Yes, reader, however strange it may seem, this is the language of an LL.D., in the Methodist Episcopal Church South, commenting upon the language of John Calvin, the founder of the Presbyterian Church!

The Doctor continues:

"In like manner, Dr. John Dick, in his learned and powerfully reasoned *Lectures on Theology*, can no more see that the baptism of infants is enjoined in the words of Matthew xxviii. 19, than could John Calvin. *Adults*, says he, *and not children*, 'are specified in this commission.' Hence the words of the commission, in themselves considered, have no bearing on the subject of infant baptism."
* * * * * * * * * *

Again:

"The Rev. J. C. Ryle is one of the latest, the most learned, and the most universally admired evangelical expositors of the Gospels, and yet where Mr. Miller sees (in Matthew xxviii. 19) 'a command for infant baptism,' this great Pedobaptist does not *see one express word in its* *favor.* * * * Hence he adds: 'I purposely abstain from saying anything on the subject of infant baptism. *There is nothing in this text* (Matthew xxviii. 19) which can be fairly used either way in settling this much vexed controversy.'"

The Doctor adds:

"It is incumbent on Mr. Miller 'to show a command for infant baptism,' to Presbyterians and Methodists, to the followers of Calvin and Wesley, and open their eyes to see it, before he tries his novel 'method of proof' on the Baptists."

Yes, neither Presbyterians, with all their learning, nor Methodists, with all their ardent zeal, have ever seen, according to Dr. Bledsoe (and of course he knows), in this, or any other text, a command to baptize infants.

Is it a wonder, then, that Baptists have never seen it either?

In taking the testimony of one, the testimony of several Pedobaptists has been obtained. They all agree that the commission has nothing whatever to do with infant baptism, but refers to adults exclusively—*the very thing contended for all along.* Remember *that;* and then remember also that the commission is the *only authority* on record for baptizing any one, even adults. Then what becomes of infant baptism? Is it not devoid of any support from divine authority? If it is not in the commission, then it is no where. That it is not in the commission, its very best friends abundantly and emphatically concede and show. They endeavor, of course, to meet the difficulty. In the same issue of the *Southern Review,** as quoted

---
* P. 177.

above, appears a paragraph, not in the same article, but from the same pen, which shows how keenly this difficulty is felt by Pedobaptists, and how they attempt to meet it. For the sake of convenience and to avoid repetition, in quoting the language, some insertions will be made, designated, in every case, however, by the brackets, which are used for that purpose. The following is the sentence from Dr. Bledsoe's ready pen:

"We object to the bold statement of Mr. Miller, that Matthew xxviii. 19, 'is the only authority we have for administering baptism to any one.' For if so [and it has never been, nor can it be successfully contradicted, for where is any other to be found?], *then we have no authority whatever for administering baptism to infants* [and that is exactly the case], since Matthew xxviii. 19 [unquestionably our only authority to baptize] does not say one word about infants, and *can not be extended to infants,* unless you look beyond the words themselves for our authority to do so.* Hence, in confining our authority for baptism to these words alone [which all are compelled to do], he has betrayed the cause of infant baptism into the hands of its

---

* But what right have you to extend the *meaning* or *authority* of the commission even by looking beyond the words themselves? For the authority is contained *only in the words.* Certainly every means should be used; the surroundings of a text should be carefully and prayerfully studied in order to know the *meaning* of the text—in this case to learn what Christ *meant* and *authorized* by this commission. But by no means can that *meaning* or that *authority* be *extended,* so as to include more than was intended by the inspired writer. Take one of Dr. Bledsoe's examples: " God commanded Joshua to make sharp knives and to circumcise again the children of Israel." You may look beyond these words to the custom of that people, simply to learn their meaning and *the extent of their authority.* And when that is know, we dare not, we can not go beyond it, *or extend* it. So with the commission. The words must be studied; and so the surroundings. Learn what it *authorizes;* and then to extend that authority to infants, even by looking beyond the words themselves, is impossible and absurd, if Christ did not include them. But this Dr. Bledsoe denies.

enemies. Are not the numerous—we had almost said the innumerable—instances of baptism, in the New Testament, some authority for the administration of this rite? [Certainly not, except as they derive their authority from the commission—*our only authority* to baptize] Are not," he continues, "the words of Mark xvi 16, 'He that believeth and is baptized shall be saved,' some authority for the importance as well as for the existence of the rite of baptism?"

Certainly, these words *show* " the *importance,*" and *show* " *the existence,*" and they may be some " *authority* for the *administration* of the rite" of baptism. But why this sudden change of terms —" importance as well as existence," instead of " administration of the rite "—in the Doctor's language? But it is no matter, for the words of Mark are simply a different version of the *same* commission given in Matthew xxviii. 19—OUR ONLY AUTHORITY TO BAPTIZE. And, besides, if it was another commission, surely no support is offered to the cause of infant baptism by such words—" he that *believeth* and is baptized." And, furthermore, the " numerous instances of baptism recorded in the New Testament," are not the least authority for the administration of baptism. Why is not the " community of goods " binding upon the churches of to-day? Because that was a temporary provision, which the disciples, guided no doubt, however, by the Holy Spirit, devised for the pinching exigencies of those special times. And it passed away, therefore, with the necessity that gave it being. Not so, however, with the baptisms they performed and left on record. These were administered under the direct authority, or in obedience to the direct command of the Lord Jesus Christ. This command was given in the commission; where Christ not only authorized but also *perpetuated* to "the end of the world" this sacred ordinance. Under this command the disciples acted *then*, and under this command the disciples of the same Savior act *now*. Christ's ministers to-day have their authority to administer the ordinance of baptism, not at second-hand from the apostles, but from the same source with them— viz: from the *commission*. Leave that, and no where can you find a command or any authority to baptize. While the baptisms performed by the apostles, and their co-laborers, may serve as examples to us, showing the extent of the authority given by Christ; yet they are themselves not the least authority for us to baptize. Hence, again, the necessity for abiding by the commission of our Master.

Now, mark you, in the last quotation given from Dr. Bledsoe, he admits, and it is the admission of a master mind, that if the commission "contains our only authority for baptizing, then is *infant* baptism betrayed into the hands of its ememies," and there is "no authority whatever for administering baptism to infants, since Matthew xxviii. 19 does not say one word about infants, and can not be extended to infants." It therefore devolves upon Pedobaptists to show another command, or some other authority, outside of this, for baptizing, which will include the infant as well as the believing adult. This demand is reasonable and just. And until they do this, their cause has not the least sanction in the word of God. Pedobaptists themselves being the judges, the commission certainly contains no authority for the baptism of infants. This is all that is contended for now. And in conceding this, they have, with their own hands, removed the very foundation-stone upon which rested every pillar that supports the whole superstructure of the Pedobaptist theory. *And a crash is inevitable.* Their time-honored temple—

> " With gilded roofs and towers of stone,
> Now instant all around,
> With sudden *crash* and dreadful groan,
> Rushes thundering to the ground."

The labor done by the apostles and their co-laborers, such as preaching the gospel, baptizing, etc., they did under the authority of *this* commission. Their doings, therefore, may be considered as a manifestation of its practical workings, showing how it was understood by those to whom it was immediately given, and who were so miraculously guided by the Holy Spirit that they could not err in its interpretation. To the Acts of the Apostles, therefore, and to the Epistles so far as they bear upon this subject, your attention is now called.

But let it be distinctly restated, and ever remembered, that this is done, not for the purpose of finding, there, authority to baptize, but simply to learn how the commission was understood by them. Nor is this reasoning in a circle, an appeal from the commission to the apostolic practice, and then *vice versa.* But these—their practice on the one hand, and the commission on the other—form the two sides of an arch, each supporting the other. And this gives to "believer's baptism only" a foundation, which has stood through the ages, and which still stands as solid and as immovable as the everlasting hills. About ten days after receiving the commission from their risen Lord, who immediately thereupon ascended to glory, the apostles began their labors in Jerusalem (Acts ii.), having been commanded to abide in that city "until endued with power from on high." And there they abode in an upper room, and "continued with one accord in prayer and supplication." "And suddenly there came a sound from heaven, as of a rushing mighty wind, and it filled all the house where they were sitting. And there appeared unto them cloven tongues like as of fire, and it sat upon them. And they were all filled with the Holy Spirit, and began to speak with tongues, *as the Spirit gave them utterance.*"

This was the "power from on high," the baptism in the Holy Spirit, whom Jesus, "being by the right hand of God exalted, and having received of the Father the promise of the Holy Ghost," was now shedding forth upon his disciples to be their comforter and guide amid the trials and labors that should come upon them; and who should "teach them all things, and bring all things to their remembrance, whatsoever he had said unto them." These were indeed favorable auspices under which to begin their work. Now, it is impossible for them to mistake the meaning of Christ's language. *They are filled with the Holy Spirit.*

The *first* thing the commission enjoined, and the first thing they did, was to *preach the gospel* to a large concourse of people—"devout men, from every nation under heaven"—gathered in Jerusalem to attend one of their annual feasts.

Under that sermon, many were "*pricked in their hearts,*" and cried out, "Men and brethren, what must we do?" Peter answered (see Acts ii. 38, 39). Here are the facts in the case: 1. Peter preached the gospel. 2. Some, being "pricked in their hearts," inquired what to do. 3. Peter answered: "Repent, and be baptized every one of you in the name of Jesus Christ for the remission of sins, and ye shall receive the gift of the Holy Ghost." Is there any place here for infants? Could they have the gospel preached to them? Could they be pricked in their hearts—*convicted of sin?* Could they be, with any reason, commanded to *repent?* Could infants be baptized *in* the name of Jesus Christ? or *for the remission of sins*—whatever be the meaning of "for?" Could unintelligent infants, upon their baptism, receive the gift of the Holy Ghost? And yet baptism is connected with all of these things. Who were baptized? "Then they that *gladly received* the word" (*i. e.*, believed the gospel just preached) "were baptized." (Verse 41.) Pedobaptism is wholly unknown here. Let him find it who can. As the expression, "The promise is unto you and your *children,*" though formerly considered as one of their strong proof-texts, is now abandoned by many able Pedobaptists, as in no sense bearing upon infant baptism, it may be passed over with a single remark. The word *children* is used not in the sense of *babes* of those parents then present, but of *posterity* simply. This is a common use of the word. Remember, too, that to these children is the *promise* of the Holy Spirit; and these the Lord our God shall call. Now, when it comes to pass that a babe can receive the miraculous gifts of the Spirit, and can hear the calling of God, it will be time enough then to give this text a further notice. It is not at all strange that Dr. Whitby,* a Pedobaptist, would write as follows:

"These words will not prove a right of infants to receive baptism, the *promise* here being that of the Holy Ghost mentioned in verses 16, 17, 18, and so *relating only* to the times of the miraculous effusions [?] of the Holy Ghost, and to those persons *who by age were capable of these extraordinary gifts.*"

Albert Barnes on this passage says:

"It does not refer to children *as children*, and should not be adduced to establish the propriety of infant baptism, or as applicable particularly to infants. It is a promise, indeed, to parents that the *blessings of salvation* shall not be confined to parents, but shall be extended to their posterity."

And so other Pedobaptists could be quoted, but it is useless. For no one, in this age of improved biblical exegesis and interpretation, would venture to found an argument on this passage for infant baptism—unless, forsooth, his cause was in the last

---

*Quoted in Howell's Evils of Infant Baptism, p. 48.

desperate struggle. If Christ, in giving the commission, authorized infant baptism, it is most remarkable that we have no mention of the practice here, where, since the giving of the commission, the gospel was first preached, and the ordinance was administered for the first time. Moreover, *every circumstance* connected with, as also *every word* in the narrative, is irreconcilable with the practice.

And when, through persecution, the disciples were scattered abroad, they went everywhere—not, as some would have us believe, baptizing men, women, and chidren, irrespective of their age or moral preparation, as if by that to make them disciples—but "*preaching the word;*" by preaching the gospel they *made disciples*, and then baptized them as their Master had done, and had commanded them to do. Philip went to the city of Samaria, and unto the citizens of that city he "preached Christ." Notice how he follows the *order* of the commission. "And the people gave heed, hearing and seeing the miracles which were wrought." (Acts viii. 5, 6.) As infants could not, of course, be included in this first part of the work, so they can not in the other. For " When they *believe*" (or were made disciples by) "Philip preaching the kingdom of God, and the name of Jesus Christ, they" (then, just as the commission had enjoined) "were baptized, both men and women." (Acts viii. 12.) No infants here. And yet the disciples understood the commission and labored in accordance with its injunctions. Again, in the same chapter, Philip meets the Eunuch. This case subserves no purpose here, except to show the direction given in the commission. Philip preaches Jesus; the Eunuch *believes, becomes a disciple* under his preaching; then Philip baptizes him. Jesus is preached; Jesus is believed on; Jesus is obeyed. Such is the divine order. And such is the case in every example on record. Next, Peter, by invitation, visits Cornelius at his home in Cesarea. (Acts x.) Having arrived he "found many that were come together," and having heard the explanation of his being sent for, he began *preaching the gospel.* " While he yet spake these words the Holy Spirit fell on *all them that heard his word;" they were made disciples and did all magnify God.* And then Peter "commanded them to be baptized." Also (Acts xviii. 8): " And many of the Corinthians *believing were baptized."* It is worthy of remark, how, in all these examples of the apostolic practice, they uniformly followed the injunctions of the commission, even in *the order*—a matter of little importance to some of this day—in which the Savior gave them. In every instance, (1) by the preaching of the gospel, persons were made disciples, became believers in the Lord Jesus Christ, and (2) then they were baptized —put on the badge of discipleship.

The household baptisms of the New Testament are in perfect harmony with this practice. This is claimed as strong ground. And by their bold assertions, Pedobaptists seem to think that even intelligent persons will believe that one example of infant baptism has really been found. But with the most diligent searching, they have been unable to produce *one single infant* from all these households. It is to argue wildly and fallaciously, that because households were baptized, therefore infants are baptized. The argument is completely overthrown by simply asking are there not numbers of households in which there is not a single infant? It must be *proved* beyond all doubt; it will not do to *assume* that the households mentioned had infants among their number. In the New Testament there are two households mentioned as believing, with nothing said of their baptism. (John iv. 53, and Acts xviii. 8.) There are two others whose baptism, as well as their faith, is mentioned. There is one other whose baptism is spoken of, but nothing is said about their faith. The most superficial thinker would naturally supply the faith where it was not mentioned in the one, just as they would the baptism where it was not mentioned in the other cases.

The baptism of the Philippian jailer and his household is recorded in Acts xvi. 31–34. On reading the narrative you will observe the following facts: 1. Paul and Silas "spake unto him the word of the Lord, and to *all that were in his house.*" 2. And then baptized "him and all his, immediately." 3. And having brought Paul and Silas into his house (he had previously taken them out to wash their stripes and was baptized while out), the jailer " set meat before them, and *rejoiced, believing in God with all his house.*" Were there any infants in this household, think you? Could they be spoken to, *i. e.*, have the gospel preached unto them? Do you candidly believe that unintelligent infants were made disciples by the preaching of the gospel? That they became *believers* in the Lord Jesus Christ, and *believing* were baptized? That they *rejoiced, believing in God?*" You DO? What! that there were infants in the jailer's household, and were baptized? And that these *same infants* certainly *heard the gospel, believed it, and rejoiced?* Verily, then, they were extraordinary infants!!

A Pedobaptist commentator, Bloomfield, says:

"It is taken for granted that his family *became Christians* as well as himself."

It is childish to talk of infant baptism in this household. Nothing but the greatest extremity would force one to take shelter under it. Here, as in all the other narratives, there is an inspired commentary on the commission. 1. The gospel is preached, and by it men are made disciples—become believers. 2. Then as believers they are baptized. A contrary case can not be found in all the New Testament. These men were guided by God's unerring Spirit. Hence, the uniformity of their practice.

CHAPTER V.

THERE was also the household of Stephanas, who were baptized by Paul. (1 Corinthians i. 16.) But, most unquestionably, there were no infants among them. For in the same Epistle (xvi. 15) it is distinctly said: "Ye know the household of Stephanas, *that it was the first-fruits of Achaia, and that they have addicted themselves to the ministry of the saints.*" It will be time enough to give this case a further notice, when it has been proved, or when it is even thought, that unintelligent babes can be *converted*, or in any sense can be the *fruit, the result of*, or *made disciples* by, the preaching of the gospel, and when it shall be further shown that infants can addict themselves to the ministry, to the waiting on, or the attending to, the saints. This household of Stephanas was the *first-fruits* of the apostolic preaching in Achaia, the first in that heathen land, who, by the preaching of the gospel, had been *persuaded* to turn from their idols, to serve the true and living God, and these converts had given themselves to the ministry of the saints.

And now comes the "STRONGHOLD" of Pedobaptism, viz: the baptism of LYDIA and HER HOUSEHOLD. (Acts xvi. 13–15, 40.) Her "heart the Lord opened, that she attended unto the things which were spoken of Paul," while he sat by the river side, "and spake" (or preached the gospel) "unto the women which resorted thither." Lydia and others were converted under the sermon. "And when she was baptized, and her household, she besought us, saying, If ye have judged me to be faithful to the Lord, come unto my house, and abide." This verse is claimed to support the dogma of infant baptism. It is constantly asserted and reasserted, over and over again, that this household was baptized upon the faith of Lydia. To which, however, it is sufficient to reply, that the Scriptures say no such thing. The language does not even *imply*, much less *necessitate*, such an intrepretation. Should it be said, " when Mrs. A was baptized, and her husband, she prevailed on the ministers to stop at her house," would any one suppose that the husband had been baptized upon the wife's faith? Why then suppose, in a similar case of construction, that Lydia's *house* was baptized on *her* faith? If this be the meaning, then it would follow that so soon as the wife was converted and baptized, her husband, no matter how wicked and immoral in life; all her children, no matter as to either their age or moral standing; and all the servants, no difference either how *old*, or how wicked, or how profligate, they may be; these all must be at once baptized upon the faith of the wife, the mother, the mistress! Take the position that Lydia's household were baptized upon her faith, and this conclusion is inevitable: you **must** either abandon the position or accept with it the conclusion. Which will *you* do? Baptists say "every man must give an account of *himself* unto God." But even admitting that they were baptized upon her faith, which is not done, it by no means follows that there were *infants* in her house, or that infants were baptized. How do you know there were any infants there? This must be clearly established before the passage can be of the least avail to Pedobaptists. To *prove* this they *assume* (1) that Lydia was married; (2) that she had children; (3) that these children were all infants; (4) that she had them with her at Philippi, *three hundred miles* from her home in Thyatira. These are all necessary adjuncts to the argument, and yet are all merely gratuitous assumptions— none of them are probable, but are all *improbable! Four baseless assumptions!* Do four *ciphers*, added together, make anything? So certainly, do four *improbable assumptions prove nothing.*

No one doubts that Lydia was baptized upon a profession of her faith. And in view of the commission, which commanded the baptism of believers, and all the former actions of the apostles, baptizing only upon a profession of a *personal* faith in a *personal* Savior, who can reasonably doubt, this household, like those persons at Corinth and other places, "*believing*, were baptized?" The baptism of Crispus' household is not questioned, because it is not mentioned, it being stated simply that they *believed.* Of course they would be baptized as they were disciples or believers. In the case of

Lydia's household, however, nothing is said about their believing, but only they were baptized. It was not necessary to mention their faith. If it were said of a certain Baptist minister that he had baptized a number of persons, would you suppose that he had baptized some who were not *professed* believers, simply because the fact of their believing is not mentioned? The apostles, in their day, were not more uniform in the practice of baptizing only *professed disciples* or *believers*, than are the Baptists to-day. The very fact that a Baptist minister has baptized an individual is full evidence that such an individual had made a profession of faith. So in the case of those baptized by the apostles. If nothing had been said about Lydia, except what is contained in verse fifteen, "And when she was baptized," etc., no one would doubt for a moment that she had believed. Why doubt about the household? The very fact that they were baptized is evidence sufficient that they were *believers* or *disciples*.

Dr. De Witt, a Pedobaptist, feeling the force of this, in his commentary* on the passage, says:

" This passage has been adduced in proof of the apostolical authority of infant baptism, but there is no proof here that any except adults were baptized."

Dr. Olshausen, a German Pedobaptist, also says in his commentary † on the New Testament:

"There is no trace to be found here of instruction before baptism [is it possible that he overlooked the fact

---
* Baptist Short Method, p. 109.
† In hoc loco.

that Paul had preached the gospel to Lydia and the rest of them, verse xiv.?]; without doubt, the rite took place *merely* on a *profession of faith in Jesus as the Messiah.* But for that *very reason* it is *highly improbable* that the phrase (*oikos autes*), *her household*, should be understood as including *infant children.*"

See how a learned Pedobaptist expresses himself on this passage. He excludes infants, and does it upon the precise ground as the Baptists do, viz: because "*it took place merely upon a profession of faith in Jesus as the Messiah.*" And then in this immediate connection, and right under the shadow of the " strong (?) hold of Pedobaptism," the same distinguished writer adds:

"*There is altogether wanting any conclusive proof-passage for the baptism of children in the age of the apostles, nor can the necessity of it be drawn from the nature of the ordinance.*"

That those composing her household were not infants, but believers, is confirmed by what is said in verse forty of the same chapter. Paul and Silas " went out of the prison, and entered into the house of Lydia, and when they had seen the *brethren*, they *comforted* them, and departed." Here her household, the first converts of that famous city, are called *brethren* and are *comforted*. Can infants be classed among such? Can they receive the comforts of the gospel? Would *you* call them "the brethern?" Do *you* believe that there were infants among those *comforted brethren* in *Lydia's household?*

It is all in vain to say that these were Paul's traveling companions. Only *three* persons went with him to this chief city of Macedonia. Silas, one of these, is in prison with him. Luke, another one of them, in writing the record says: "Paul and Silas went out of the prison and," not *came* (as he would have put it, if he had been in the house at the time) but "*entered* into the house of Lydia, and *comforted*" (not *us*, as he would have said, had he been among them, but) *the brethren*, who were in the house. Most likely, therefore, Luke was not in the house at the time, and, consequently, not among those whom Paul *comforted*. Where Timothy, the only remaining companion, was, it is not stated. But surely the inspired historian would not call him "*the brethren*." Perhaps Timothy, and Lydia, and her *infant children*, were the *comforted brethren !!!* But who were they? If we must infer, surely " the most reasonable inference is that her household consisted of persons in her employ, that *they believed* and were baptized as well as Lydia, and that they were '*the brethren*' whom Paul and Silas *comforted*, when released from prison they 'entered into the house of Lydia.'"

This household baptism has been considered the strongest example for infant baptism that can be furnished by all the practice of the apostles. And yet there is no evidence, *absolutely none*, that there were any infants there; while there is proof positive on the other hand that there was simply the baptism of believers. Before these New Testament household baptisms can, in the least, advantage Pedobaptists, it must be established beyond the shadow of a doubt, either (1) that in *every* household there are infants; or (2) that in those mentioned here—of the jailer, of Stephanas, and Lydia—there were most unquestionably infants to be found. The first has never been attempted. For there are scores of households all over this country—many of them in *Baptist* churches—in which there is not a single infant.

It is a thing of common occurrence for Baptist ministers to baptize households, as did the apostles, but they do not baptize infants.

To establish the second of these, some have tried, but most signally failed. The *only evidence* that infants were baptized, is that *households* are mentioned—and this is no evidence at all, not even presumptive evidence. The fallacy in the argument is perfectly patent. For many Baptist ministers, both in this country and foreign lands, have baptized more *households* than are mentioned in the New Testament, and have so reported. But is any one either so ignorant, or so insane, as to infer from the reading of household baptisms, in these reports, that therefore infants were baptized by Baptist ministers?

On the other hand, Baptists have gone further than could be required of them, and shown conclusively that these households, in the New Testament, were all *believing* households; that "facts and circumstances are related which render it a moral certainty that there were no infants in those baptized families." There is not a single baptism mentioned in the New Testament, but what, in connection with it, some statement is made that necessitates the exclusion of the unintelligent babe. Indeed, the concessions made by some able Pedobaptists concerning household baptisms have utterly broken the force of the arguments drawn from them by others.

In Kitto's Biblical Eyclopedia* is an article on baptism, prepared by Professor J. Jacobi, at the request of Neander, and indorsed by him ' as in unison with his own principles." Alluding to household baptisms, as the "*strongest* argument" from scripture for infant baptism, the writer says, however, that:

" In none of these instances has it been proved that there were little children among them; but even supposing that there were, there was no necessity for excluding them from baptism by plain words, *since such an exclusion was understood as a matter of course.*"

Neander† himself says:

" We can not infer the existence of infant baptism from instances of the baptism of whole families, for the passage, 1 Corinthians xvi. 15, shows the fallacy of such a conclusion, as from that it appears that the whole family of Stephanas, who were baptized by Paul, consisted of adults."

From Coleridge, who stands among Pedobaptists second neither to Neander nor Jacobi, the same work‡ gives also the following quotations:

" I must concede to you that too many of the Pedobaptists have erred. * * * If I should inform any one that I had called at a friend's house, but had found nobody at home, the family having all gone to the play; and if he,

---

* Curtis' Prog. Bapt. Prin. p. 93.
† Same, p. 94.
‡ P. 94.

on the strength of the information, should take occasion to asperse my friend's wife, for unmotherly conduct in taking an infant, six months' old, to a crowded theater, would you allow him to press the words 'no body' and 'all the family' in justification of the slander? Would you not tell him that the words were to be interpreted by the nature of the subject, the purpose of the speaker, and their ordinary acceptation; and that he must or might have known that infants of that age would not be admitted to the theater? Exactly so with regard to the words, '*he and all his household.*' Had the baptism of infants at that early period of the gospel been a known practice, or had this been previously demonstrated, then, indeed, the argument that in all probability there were infants or young children in so large a family, would be no otherwise objectionable than as *being superfluous,* and a *sort of anti-climax in logic.* But if the words are cited as the proof it would be a clear *petitio principis,* though there had been nothing else against it. *But when we turn back to the Scriptures preceding the narrative and find repentance and belief demanded as the terms and* INDISPENSABLE CONDITIONS *of baptism, then the case above imagined applies in its full force."*

Will you not, with these learned Pedobaptists, abandon the *households* of the New Testament, and never mention them again in connection with *infant baptism?* In all the practice of the apostles, who no doubt understood the law of baptism, as through the four Gospels, there is *nothing* to show this to be from heaven or a divine appointment. The whole ground, so far, has been surrendered, step by step, by Pedobaptists themselves.

The Epistles now remain.

In connection with these there are *two facts*—the one renders it *improbable,* the other *impossible,* that Pedobaptism was a thing known, much less practiced, by the apostles or the apostolic churches.

The *first* is, that throughout the Epistles, not one word is said about "the children of the covenant," "the baptized children of the church;" "their covenant relations," or any such phrases which abound in the service and in the prayers of Pedobaptists, as well as in their literature. This is remarkably singular upon the hypothesis that Pedobaptism was them practiced. Verily, the apostles were censurably neglectful of the "little lambs of the fold!" "Would a Pedobaptist apostle have pursued this course? To bring the matter nearer home, would a Pedobaptist missionary write a letter to a Pedobaptist Church—making special mention of parents and children, urging both to a faithful performance of relative duties—and say nothing of the obligations of either parents or children, as connected with, or growing out of infant baptism?" Of course not. And yet this is just the course pursued by the inspired writers of the New Testament.

The *second* fact is, that these same writers, in addressing the churches, used terms which are absolutely inadmissible as being applicable to unconscious babes. *E. g.*, "*Faithful brethern*," "*The called in Christ Jesus*," "*Called to be saints*," and such kindred terms, which abound in the Epistles, and will be readily remembered by those familiar with them. Certainly these terms can not be applied to infants. And, besides, those who were baptized are spoken of in such a way as to make it impossible for *infants* to have been among them. " Paul refers to the '*baptized*,' as 'dead to sin '—as rising from the baptismal waters to 'walk in newness of life'—as 'putting on Christ'—as 'risen with him through the faith of the operation of God'—as 'baptized for the dead,' or in the *belief* of the resurrection—as making a 'profession of faith,' a 'profession before many witnesses,' etc. These phrases are utterly destitute of meaning if applied to unintelligent babes." Are these *facts* without a most significant bearing on the question—"Is it from heaven or of man?" Is not this the natural conclusion, that Pedobaptism, or infant membership, was not thought of, by either the apostles or the apostolic churches, and are therefore of human origin? Can this be fairly denied? There is one passage which perhaps ought to be referred to in this connection, viz: 1 Corinthians vii. 14, "Else were your children unclean, but now are they holy." Read carefully the entire context, and *you* will see that there is not the slightest allusion to baptism, either of adults or of infants. The case is simply this: the question is asked, shall there be a separation of husband and wife where one is a believer and the other an unbeliever? Shall the believing husbands and wives put away their unbelieving partners? No, says Paul, you can not do that, for by such an action you would prove *your own* children (whose parents are in the church) unclean, *i. e.* ceremonially, illegitimate before the law, and they must be put away also, on the same ground. But now are *your* children (*i. e.*, *of believing parents*) holy, *ceremonially* clean, *legitimate before the law*, and of course, therefore, they must not be cast off. Neither must the unbelieving husband and wife be put away for they sustain to their unbelieving partners, the *same relation* as children sustain to their believing parents. "The passage is intensely strong against infant baptism. It shows that children of the members of the Corinthian Church sustained the same relation to the church that unbelieving husbands and wives did, and that if believing husbands and wives abandoned their unbelieving partners, believing parents might, with the same propriety, separate themselves from their children." This is manifestly the apostle's argument to show that the believer must not put away the unbelieving partner. (Verses 12 and 13.) He classes in the same category children of believing parents, and the unbelieving husband or wife whose partner is a believer. And one may be baptized with as much propriety as the other

On this passage Albert Barnes, in his commentary, says :

"There is not one word about baptism here, not one allusion to it, nor does the argument in the remotest degree bear upon it The question was not whether children should be baptized, but it was whether there should be a separation between man and wife, where the one was a Christian and the other not. Paul states that *if* such a separation should take place, it would imply that the marriage was improper, and, of course, the children must be regarded as unclean."

Olshausen, also, in his commentary on the text, says:

"It is moreover clear, that Paul would not have chosen

this line of argument had infant baptism been at that time practiced."

Professor Jacobi, in the article on baptism previously quoted, says :*

"A pretty sure indication of its (infant baptism) non-existence in the apostolic age may be inferred from 1 Corinthians vii. 14, since Paul would certainly have referred to the baptism of the children for their holiness."

The *North British Review*, a Presbyterian journal of Scotland, and edited by Dr. Hanna, is quoted by Curtis in the same work,† as containing in its August number, 1852, the following:

"1 Corinthians vii. 14, is incompatible with the supposition that infant baptism was then practiced at Corinth. * * * Many, indeed, have explained the term holy as meaning 'have been admitted to baptism,' making the verse say that if the faith of the unbelieving partner had not sanctified the marriage, the children would not have been admitted to baptism, whereas they had been baptized. *But this is to re-write Scripture, not to interpret it.*"

Must it be repeated that these four men, Barnes, Olshausen, Jacobi, and Hanna (to whom could have been added others), are all learned Pedobaptists, and of good standing in their churches? Yet they declare in the most emphatic language that the passage, 1 Corinthians vii. 14, has not a thing to do with baptism.

The New Testament, in which is to be found the *whole law* of Christian baptism, has been diligently searched; not in all the sayings of Christ, not in

---
*Curtis' Prog. Bapt. Prin. p. 96.
†P. 97.

all the doings and sayings of the apostles, not in the commission, where the ordinance was instituted, and the law given by which the ordinance was to be controlled; not in all the *inspired commentary* on that commission, found in the Acts of the Apostles, *nowhere from Matthew to Revelation*, one single precept, or example, or even "*one word*," has been found to justify the baptism of unintelligent infants. The Pedobaptist world has been challenged time and again; they have been offered large rewards to produce from the New Testament, *just one* precept or example for the practice. But they have never produced it. It can not be found.

Hence, Colridge, in Curtis' work* already quoted, says:

"I confine myself to the assertion—not that infant baptism was not—but there is no sufficient proof that it was the practice of the apostolic age."

And Neander, also quoted by the same writer,† says:

"*It is certain that Christ did not ordain infant baptism. We can not prove that the apostles ordained it.*"

Julius Mueller, quoted by Dr. Alvah Hovey, in *Baptist Quarterly*,‡ and called by him "one of the ablest theologians of Germany," says:

"According to the very idea of baptism it supposes, besides the external act, a person who *receives the same with faith* in the promise of Jesus Christ, *and confesses this faith;*

---
*P. 97.
†P. 103.
‡For April, 1875, p. 139.

and this presupposes an antecedent *preaching of the word of Christ to him*. The scriptural proofs for the necessity of infant baptism are *untenable*. * * * The fact that new-born children were baptized by the apostles can in *no way* be shown; on the contrary, the manner in which the *apostles everywhere* speak of baptism, *together with* 1 *Corinthians vii*. 14, and the *narratives of the oldest church history*, PUT IT BEYOND DOUBT THAT INFANT BAPTISM HAD NO PLACE IN THE APOSTOLIC CHURCH."

And he a Pedobaptist! The wonders under heaven are numerous indeed! By *what authority* is this thing done? Is this practice from heaven or of men? In the next chapter other learned advocates of the practice may give their further testimony to this question.

But, dear readers, together we have gone through the New Testament, and now what think *you* of the subject? Suffer a few *personal* questions. It is no desire on the part of the writer to sustain a theory, simply for the theory's sake. (O blessed Redeemer, if my cause is not thy cause, let it *perish*, that *truth may be established!*) Were you baptized in infancy? Then in the name of Him who loved us, and gave Himself for us, may it be asked: In the light of all the facts presented in the foregoing pages, have *you* been baptized *by the authority* (where can the authority be found), and INTO *the name, of the adorable Trinity?* Was *your baptism*, administered when you knew nothing of it, a *profession of your faith* in Christ? the answer of *your conscience*, then made good by regeneration, *toward God?* Did *your conscience, then*, demand of *you* this act of obedience; and did *you*, at that time *in your infancy*, submit to *that ordinance in response to the demand made by your conscience?* All these questions you must answer in the negative. Then you have not been baptized, have never obeyed Christ in this ordinance. True, it is a trial—a *severe* trial—to renounce the baptism given by your father and your mother. But remember the words of the Crucified One: "He that loveth father or mother more than me *is not worthy of me;*" and also those other fearful words: "For if we sin *willfully* after that we have received the knowledge of the truth, there remaineth no more sacrifice for sins; but a fearful looking for of judgment and fiery indignation."

The words of Cotton Mather are commendable words: "Let a precept be never so difficult, or never so distasteful to flesh and blood, yet if I see it is God's command, my soul says, It is good; let me obey it, till I die."

"If a man love me, he will keep my words, and my Father will love *him*, and we will come unto him, and make our abode with *him*." Can you, dear friend, claim this blessed promise? Do you *love* the Savior? "He that hath my commandments, and *keepeth them*, he it is that loveth me." "If ye *love me*, keep my commandments," *all of them*. This is the language of Him to whom we expect to sing among the redeemed in glory: "Unto him that loved *us*, and washed us from our sins, in his own blood, and hath made us kings and priests unto God and his Father; to him be glory and dominion forever and ever. Amen."

CHAPTER VI.

In the New Testament is given a full account of the institution of the churches of Christ; the rules by which they are governed; the two ordinances, Baptism and the Lord's Supper; and, of all the regulations for the administration of them.

Baptism is a New Testament ordinance. But after a most diligent examination of that volume, not a single command, not a single example, not even one word has been found to support the dogma of *infant* baptism. Here the matter might rest. The question is decided. Infant baptism is of men. It has no sanction in the word of God. Still, however, it is believed in and practiced by a large number of good people. And they have a variety of arguments that at least seem to them to sustain it. Without entering upon an investigation or formal refutation of these, there are two considerations, which deepen the belief that it is of men, and manifestly show that there must be a flaw and an evident weakness in the arguments by which it is defended, and upon the strength of which it is practiced. The one is, *that nearly all the arguments advanced in its favor, can be urged with equal propriety and equal force in support of* INFANT COMMUNION, viz: the *antiquity of that practice:* the *Lord's Supper* in the room of the Passover, of which feast infants partook; the *silence* of the New Testament—infant communion is not forbidden, etc., etc. This is significant. Now, all these arguments, with their irresistible (?) power, equal to the emergency in the case of *infant baptism*, have led no one, in modern times, to the practice of *infant communion*. They force to the one, but not to the other! Nor were Pedobaptists prevented from abandoning the practice of *infant communion*, by the same arguments by which they now defend *infant baptism*. The two dogmas are of near kin as well as near the same age. Baptism and the Supper, as instituted by Christ, rest upon the same authority —*positive law*. And both are to be preserved in their sacred and primitive purity. And is it not singular that the *same arguments*, which admit the unintelligent infants to the one, will not admit them to the other! This very fact is a manifestation of the weakness of the arguments. And, moreover, there is not a single objection, which can be raised against *infant communion*, but what the *same*, or a kindred objection, can be raised against *infant baptism*. Why practice one and not the other? The *other* consideration, and the one especially to be noticed in this chapter, is: These arguments, if not entirely demolished, are greatly weakened by the *concessions of many of the ablest Pedobaptists themselves to the effect*, THAT IN ALL THE NEW TESTAMENT THERE IS NOT ONE PRECEPT OR EXAMPLE, OR EVEN A WORD ABOUT INFANT

BAPTISM—THAT ON THIS SUBJECT THE NEW TESTAMENT, ALTHOUGH CONTAINING THE WHOLE LAW OF BAPTISM, IS PERFECTLY SILENT. If it was not taught, nor commanded, nor practiced by either Christ or his inspired apostles, can there be any argument, of sufficient strength or plausibility, to lead to the practice of this human rite, and thereby bring ourselves under the withering curse of *adding* to the oracles of God? These concessions—and their name is legion—are indeed a heavy burden for Pedobaptists to carry in making their defense. And it is no wonder that under them, they become restive, and so strenuously endeavor to break their force, when pressed upon them by their opponents. Nor have they always used the most honorable means, or acted in the most becoming way, in their attempts to do this. But notwithstanding all their attempts to explain, and to remove this difficulty, still the burden hangs heavily. More than once has it been charged by these restless parties, that Baptists quote these concessions out of their connection, and in that way do not give the full sense of the author quoted. Is it meeting *such a charge* in language too strong to denounce it as false? especially, when it has never been sustained? Every quotation which has been given, or shall hereafter be given, either in this or succeeding chapters, will bear the most scrutinizing test of even those most competent to judge, and who are most anxious to relieve their cause of this heavy and annoying burden. (Of course you have read what is said in the "Prefatory Note" on this subject.) Do not, therefore, bring this charge against any of these quotations—at least until *you* have examined the *original* works and know for *yourself*. And when you have examined, you will find in every case, that although these men practice, and are earnest advocates for, infant baptism, yet the fact which they concede— *that the New Testament is silent on the subject*— still stands just as it is here quoted, without the least perversion or misrepresentation. And in many instances the concession will become stronger the further you examine—as it required too much space to quote more extensively than simply to get the testimony of the author to a fact. Indeed, so *profound has been this silence,* as considered by some, that they have taken *it* for the *strongest foundation* upon which to build arguments to sustain this practice!! Away, too, with every charge that bears against the piety, honesty, integrity, or scholarship of the men, from whom these concessions are taken. All of them are scholars; many of them the very salt of the Pedobaptist denominations. It is a shame that their colleagues would stoop to bring such a charge against them for doing what every reader of the Bible is forced to do. But these charges have been made against them, by their own brethren. And in doing so the person or persons have thereby rendered themselves unworthy of notice, and shown themselves in every way inferior to the men against whom they presumed to speak. Here is the difficulty—it must have been noticed by all who have read on the subject: *Pedobaptists have never been agreed among themselves as to how or where infant baptism had its rise, or was taught.* What one has built up, another with ruthless hands has torn down. What one calls his "*solid basis,*" his "*Gibraltar position,*" another, of his own faith, and equal to him, utterly destroys, by one sweeping assertion, "that it has not a thing to do with the subject." Then on the ruins of his brother's tower, *so grandly proportioned* (*!*), he begins, in turn, to lay his foundations and to build thereupon. But all too soon; the structure he has reared meets with a similar fate, from some over-earnest and confident friend. There is a very striking example of this kind of procedure in the *Southern Review** (referred to in Chapter II.), published in St. Louis, under the auspices and the indorsement of *the last* General Conference of the Methodist Episcopal Church South. The editor, Rev. A. T. Bledsoe, LL.D., gives us two articles, *the one* a review of Mr. Miller's little book in favor of infant baptism; *the other* a reply to strictures made by Mr. Miller, upon an article which the editor published in a previous issue of the *Review*. Some quotations have been, and others will be given from these articles. For the present it is sufficient to say that these two Methodist divines have the infant rite between them, and are *crushing* out its very life. Thus the matter has gone on, until every argument, and every passage of Scripture

---

*For July, 1874.

ever thought to support infant baptism, has been abandoned by one or more Pedobaptist divines. This no doubt was noticed in the preceding pages.

In the examination of every Scripture which has ever been quoted as supporting the theory, Pedobaptist authorities were given to the effect—that the passage had nothing at all to do with the subject. This same thing will be done when in the following pages some other arguments are considered. The words of the sainted John L. Waller will ever stand as immovable as the old surf-beaten rock in mid-ocean:

"No Pedobaptist has ever adduced a passage sufficiently obvious to satisfy the consciences of his brethren. Every text of Scripture ever brought to prove this doctrine, has been shown by Pedobaptists themselves not to prove it at all! We challenge the production of one exception. [This challenge, though originally printed in capital letters, and of such long standing, has met with no response!] With their own hands they have pulled down their own temple, not leaving one stone upon another. They have torn up its very foundations."

What means this confusion of tongues in the building of this modern Babel? Has God put confusion among them that they should not be understood by one another? The witnesses about to be introduced, being the zealous advocates of infant baptism, are all of course biased in that way, if biased at all, and having thoroughly studied the New Testament, they will certainly give the most favorable testimony possible. Surely you will believe them. Their concessions are of two kinds: those relating to particular passages, and those relating to the New Testament as a whole. Many of the former, and a few of the latter kind, have already been given. The ones now to be given relate to the New Testament as a whole. As each witness takes the stand the simple question put to him is this: " In all of your study and searching in the *New Testament Scriptures*, have you seen there a *single command*, or an *example* for infant baptism, or are they *perfectly silent* on the subject? Give us honestly, now, *your* testimony." And here it is. Notice closely the names of the witnesses and the testimony which they bear.

Moses Stuart* says:

"Commands, or plain and certain examples, in the New Testament relative to it (infant baptism), I do not find. Nor with my views of the subject do I need them."

Dr. Wood† (in his Lectures on Infant Baptism, p. 11) says:

"It is a plain case that there is no express precept respecting infant baptism in our Sacred Writings. The proof, then, that infant baptism is a divine institution must be made out in another way."

Neander, the Church Historian (in Church History, Vol. I. p. 311), says:

" Baptism was administered at first only to *adults*, as men were accustomed to conceive of *baptism* and *faith*, as strictly connected. We have all reason for not deriving infant baptism from apostolic institution."

Limborch (in Com. Syst. Dinvin. B. 5, ch. xxii. sec. 2) says:

---

*Mode and Subjects of Baptism, p. 190.
†Quoted in Pendleton's "Three Reasons," **p. 80.**

"There is no instance which can be produced from which it may indisputably be inferred, that any child was baptized by the apostles."

Dr. Field (on the Church, p. 375) says:

"The baptism of infants is therefore named a *tradition*, because it is not expressly delivered in Scripture that the apostles did baptize infants; nor any express precept there found that they should do so."

Robert Barclay (Apology, Propo. 12) says:

"As to the baptism of infants, it is a mere human tradition, for which neither precept nor practice is to be found in the Scriptures."

Dr. Wall, who wrote the History of Infant Baptism, for which he received a vote of thanks from the assembled clergy of the English Church, says (in its Introd. pp. 1, 55):

"Among all the persons that are recorded as baptized by the apostles, there is no express mention of any infants."

The above five quotations, with their references, which it was thought best to give, are taken from the *Baptist Short Method*,[*] by Dr. E. T. Hiscox.

Dr. Hanna (in *North British Review*)[†] says:

"Scripture knows nothing of the baptism of infants."

"There is absolutely not a single trace of it to be found in the New Testament. There are passages which may be reconciled with it, if the practice can only be proved to have existed, but there is *not one word* which asserts its existence. Nay, more; it may be argued that 1 Corinthians

---

[*] Pp. 89–92.
[†] Quoted in Curtis' Prog. Bap. Principles, p. 89.

vii. 14, is incompatible with the supposition that infant baptism was then practiced at Corinth."

The same author, in a more recent work,* says:

"No express mention is made of infants in the command of Christ, which instituted this rite (baptism); no distinct case of the baptism of infants is mentioned in the sacred narrative."

How exactly this testimony agrees with the result of our investigation!

Whatever of proof may be offered, or in whatever way they attempt to make out the case, they must fail so long as there is no precept for it, no example of it, and as it was neither instituted by Christ, nor practiced by his apostles. The testimony of *eight men*, all of whom were friends to the cause, has been taken; and these are all fully competent of bearing testimony. A jury, faithful to their trust, having before them so much testimony of such high character would not hesitate a single moment to pronounce the verdict upon *any* case. Why will you hesitate here? Is there room for the shadow of a doubt? Ought any one to practice it, or in *any way* countenance or support it, as a New Testament ordinance, if there is not a single trace of it to be found in the New Testament? Ah! Is it not a fearful thing to do so? No one acquainted with the baptismal controversy will be surprised, or consider it an exaggeration, if it be stated that the number of witnesses could easily be increased to a hundred, or even hundreds, all of whom would give the *same testimony*,

---
*Life of Christ, Vol. III. p. 310.

although Pedobaptists. Whoever can, may reconcile the practice of these men with their testimony. That is none of the concern of this work. Not their *opinion*, or their *practice*, is what is now sought; but simply their *testimony* as to a question of fact. And as honest men they *testify*, with one accord, " *the Scripture knows nothing about infant baptism.*" Only one more witness will be called to the stand. His testimony may have more influence with some because it is of later date.

Put the same question to him as to the others: " In all your study and searching in the *New Testament Scriptures,* have you seen there a *single command,* or an *example* for infant baptism; or are they *perfectly silent* on the subject?"

Rev. A. T. Bledsoe (in the *Methodist Review,* a Quarterly of more than a dozen years' standing, and which has received the sanction of the General Conference *since* giving his *testimony* to this question) answers :*

" It is an article of our faith that the 'baptism of young children (infants) is in any wise to be retained in the Church, *as most agreeable to the institutions of Christ.*' But yet, with all our searching, we have been unable to find, in the New Testament, *a single express declaration* or WORD, in favor of infant baptism. We justify the rite, therefore, solely on the ground of logical inference, and not on any express word of Christ or his Apostles. This may, perhaps, be deemed by some of our readers a strange position for a pedobaptist. It is by no means, however, a singular opinion. *Hundreds of learned pedobaptists have come to the same conclusion;* ESPECIALLY SINCE THE NEW TESTAMENT HAS BEEN SUBJECTED TO A CLOSER, MORE CONSCIEN-

---

*The *Southern Review* for April, 1874, p. 334.

TIOUS, AND MORE CANDID EXEGESIS, *than was formerly practiced by controversialists.*"

Stronger testimony than this against infant baptism could not be given. It is a master stroke; and the stroke of a friend. Brutus has stabbed Cæsar. Before such a concession, it is no wonder that some of his brethren trembled for the cause of Pedobaptism. Notice the italicized words (the emphasis is mine) and is not the whole sentence a marvel; especially, coming from one generally so true to logic? He seems to be chafing under the bridle that holds him. Although neither Christ nor his apostles said one word about infant baptism, *yet he must stand true to his Church's creed*, and infant baptism must be retained in any wise. And feeling that it must have some justification, and that it has none in the words of Christ or his apostles, he "justifies the rite, therefore, *solely on the ground of logical inference.*"

"Logical inference," indeed! But how can you have a "*logical inference*," when there is not even a word from which to start? It is simply *impossible!* Without words there can be no premises; and without premises there can be no "logical inference" or conclusion. And now as there is not in the *New Testament* even a "word in favor of infant baptism," he must go outside that book—beyond the teachings of Christ and the apostles—to find his premises, from which to get his "logical inference." Would you not like to see his premises and his conclusions? And what would they be worth so far as a *New Testament* ordinance is concerned? In that book alone can you find your premises; and in it, Dr. Bledsoe says, there is not even a "WORD IN FAVOR OF INFANT BAPTISM." Reread his testimony. It will do you good. His candor and honesty are certainly commendable, even if his logic does happen to limp.

In the following number of his *Review* (pp. 229, 230) the Doctor, while ridiculing the "inductive method," as used by Mr. Miller in supporting infant baptism, says:

"And as for induction [*i. e.*, the grouping together of scriptural facts on the subject] there is absolutely no place or use for it in the proof of infant baptism [that is true, for there are no "scriptural facts" on the subject to be gathered]. As the premises in this controversy are supplied either by the *words of Scripture* [not by these surely, for in the Scriptures there is not a "word in favor of infant baptism,"], or the facts of history [nor from these, for they can not prove *that* a New Testament ordinance, about which neither Christ nor his apostles said even a "word"], so induction has nothing whatever to do with it. All we have to do, indeed, in this controversy, is to start from the *premises* already furnished to hand [but there are none furnished—they must be found in the New Testament —and yet it is conceded "WITH ALL OUR SEARCHING, WE HAVE BEEN UNABLE TO FIND IN THE NEW TESTAMENT A SINGLE EXPRESS DECLARATION OR WORD IN FAVOR OF INFANT BAPTISM." "And not on any express word of Christ or his apostles" does he found his argument, but must get the *premises* OUTSIDE THE BIBLE], and thence *infer* or *prove* the duty of infant baptism by the use of the 'deductive method.'"

Is not this a most glaring absurdity? An egregious blunder in logic? One acquainted with the writings of Dr. Bledsoe would hardly expect to find him making such a blunder. Verily, Horace was right: it is true that good old Homer does sometimes nod. Is it singular in the least that Baptists in their study of the New Testament should reach the same conclusion with Pedobaptists, that the Scriptures *are silent* concerning the baptism of infants? And does not silence become the Pedobaptists on this subject?

" But," says Dr. Bledsoe,* " what we wish, in this connection, to emphasize most particularly, is the wonderful contrast between the silence of Christ and the everlasting clamors of his Church. Though he uttered *not one express word on* the subject of infant baptism, yet, on this very subject, have his professed followers filled the world with sound and fury. The Apostles imitated his example."

And so ought Pedobaptists. Why must it be pressed upon the Baptists, *ad nauseam*, to practice a rite as of divine appointment, but about which the divine record says not one word? Is not such a course deserving of rebuke?

But the advocates of the rite rely upon *the silence* of the Scriptures to *prove* it to be from heaven! To them " the *silence* of the Savior and the Scriptures is the voice of God in thunder tones engrafting upon the gospel a human invention!" But the ears of Baptists are not so acute as to hear the *awful voice of silence* issuing a *positive command!* Silence may *forbid* but can never *command*. "The New Testament is silent about—does not *forbid*—the baptism of infants, and therefore it is right." The suppressed premise which

---

*The *Southern Review* for April, 1874, p. 336.

must be supplied and established before the argument can avail is, everything about which the New Testament is silent, or does not forbid, *is right*. It is silent about the baptism of bells, therefore the baptism of bells is right. It is silent—does not forbid—the consecration of the bastismal waters, therefore to do that is right. It does not forbid the partaking of the Lord's Supper by infants, therefore that is right. Carlstadt demanded of Luther: "Where has Christ *commanded* us to elevate the host?" Luther replied: "Where has he *forbidden* it?" It is demanded by Baptists: "Where has Christ *commanded* the baptism of infants?" It is responded by Pedobaptists: "Where has he *forbidden* it?" By such a line of argument all the wild mummeries of Rome may be as clearly and as scripturally (!!) sustained and shown to be of divine appointment as the dogma of infant baptism!!

It is too absurd to deserve comment. And he who resorts to it, is very like the drowning man grasping at a straw. And yet it is the common resort of even intelligent Pedobaptists. When Dr. Bledsoe had pressed the argument from the silence of Scripture, even Mr. Miller, a Methodist preacher, saw the weakness of the argument, and aptly responded :*

"We never knew before that absolute *silence* upon a subject, especially when that subject had *never* been mentioned, could be a 'decisive reason' for it. Let us apply this style of reasoning (?) to **adult** baptism. Suppose Christ had

---

*Quoted in the *Southern Review* for July, 1874, p. 172.

never 'ordained' adult baptism. Dr. B. says he 'did not indeed ordain infant baptism expressly.' Again, suppose 'no express word of the Apostles' had ever been spoken for it. Dr. B. says, 'We justfy the rite . . . not on any express word of Christ *or his Apostles.*' Now, we say, suppose this absolute silence reigned through the New Testament with reference to baptizing men and women, would any man of ordinary sanity imagine that this *silence* is a 'decisive reason' for baptizing men and women? This only places adult baptism where Dr. B. places infant baptism. The fact is, the argument *ex silentio* is not worth a fig, except as a purely collateral or presumptive process. If Christ never ordained the baptism of infants, and if his apostles never uttered a word in favor of it, then their silence can not be taken as a 'decisive reason' for it, any more than their silence can be taken as a 'decisive reason' for the Roman hierarchy, concerning which they uttered no word of approval."

THAT IS SO. And yet it can not be denied—nay *it is admitted*—that concerning the dogma of Pedobaptism a silence as profound as the midnight stillness of the grave reigns over every page of the divine oracles! The stillness is so profound that it becomes audible!!

Christ commands to baptize believers. Pedobaptists have added, " and their children." And have stigmatized, persecuted and put to death the followers of Jesus, simply because they prefer to "obey God rather than men." Numbers of Baptists have sealed that preference with their life blood. Until Pedobaptists can show an *example* or *command* from the Lord Jesus Christ, whom alone we obey as our only Sovereign and Lawgiver, surely they should cease to ask intelligent persons to believe this dogma.

Pedobaptism: IS IT FROM HEAVEN OR OF MEN? The question, with the foregoing facts, is left with the candid reader to answer before his God, to whom he must render account in the last great day. It is no marvel that Prof. Lange, one of the foremost of foreign Pedobaptist writers, should be forced to the conclusion that :*

"All attempts to make out infant baptism from the New Testament fail. It is totally opposed to the spirit of the apostolic age, and to the fundamental principles of the New Testament."

Amen. Then it is of men, and not from heaven.

---
*Baptist Short Method, p. 92.

CHAPTER VII.

Upon this standing question the decision has been rendered. And that decision can never be reversed. It was given by the *New Testament*. And from its decisions no appeal can be made. By close examination, and also by the most sweeping concessions of many able Pedobaptist writers, the conclusion was reached, *that in all the New Testament there is not one word in favor of infant baptism*. And so the decision stands unalterably fixed, *it is of men*. Having failed, signally and confessedly failed, to establish their practice by the New Testament, *which is the Christian's law book*, Pedobaptists have abandoned that, and turned to the Old Testament, hoping to find some relief for their hard pressed cause. It seems that they are desirous of being "entangled again with the yoke of bondage."

But in the *Westminster Confession* it is affirmed —and in this all are agreed—that: "*Baptism* is a sacrament (an ordinance) of the *New Testament*, ordained by Jesus Christ." Every question, therefore, concerning baptism, as to its action, its design and its subjects, must be referred to and settled by that book—wherein Christ has ordained it. This is certainly reasonable. And yet Pedobaptists, after subscribing to the above article of their own creed, will not abide by it, but rush to the Old Testament to learn who are the subjects of a New Testament ordinance!! And from the very fact, that the advocates of infant baptism, abandoning the teachings of Christ and the apostolic writings, seek refuge among the forms and ceremonies of Judaism, it is perfectly clear that the rite itself can not be sustained by the New Testament. "Baptism," say they, "is a New Testament ordinance, ordained by Jesus Christ." And then admit, as has been quoted over and over again, in the preceding chapters, that *infant* baptism was ordained neither by Christ nor his apostles; that there was not a trace to be found of *infant* baptism, not a word in its favor, in the New Testament. Where is the Pedobaptist who is willing to stake his cause upon the teaching of the *New Testament*, "*especially since*," as Dr. Bledsoe says, "*the New Testament has been subjected to a closer, a more conscientious, and more candid exegesis than was formerly practiced?*"

No, they turn from this and fall back upon an *assumed identity* of the Jewish Church* and the Church of Christ, and the assumption that baptism came in the room of circumcision. Dr. Rice† thus sets forth "the identity of the churches," as it is

---

*" Jewish Church " is simply a Pedobaptist phrase for the Jewish *Theocracy*, which was no *church* at all, in the strict New Testament sense of the *word*, *church*.

†Lexington Debate, page 285.

held; and to make strong language stronger, he puts each word in italics:

"The Church, then, is the same under the Jewish and Christian dispensations—the same into which God did, by positive law, put believers and their children."

The argument drawn from this in favor of infant baptism, stated in a syllogism, stands about as follows: The Christian Church is the same as the Jewish Church; infants were members in the Jewish Church; therefore infants are members in the Christian Church. Please observe; this argument, the premises being conceded, proves—what? Infant baptism? No; but infant membership. These are two very different things, though equally erroneous. What connection subsists between *infant baptism* and *infant* church-membership has never yet been determined by even Pedobaptists themselves. Some say their baptism brings them into the Church; while others say their being in the Church entitles them to baptism. So here again, as all along the line of defense, is this confusion of tongues. Dr. Samuel Miller, of Princeton, says:[*]

"The children of professing Christians are already in the Church. They were born members. Their baptism did not make them members. It was a public ratification of their membership. They were baptized because they were members."

Dr. Rice, on the other hand, says:[†]

---
[*]Pendleton's "Three Reasons," p. 55.
[†]Lex. Debate, p. 280.

"Baptism is now the *initiatory* rite, and both (infants and adults) must receive baptism. * * The conclusion appears inevitable, that they (infants) still have the right to be in the Church, and of course to *enter* by the door—Christian baptism."

That is, entering through the door of baptism into the Church, they are members because they have been baptized. Other authorities, speaking equally *ex cathedra*, and equally antagonistic, could be quoted. Indeed Matthew Henry can be quoted on both sides of this question. Is it not a little singular, to say the least, that Pedobaptists can not agree among themselves upon one settled, deffinite reason for baptizing infant children? Some baptize them because they are in the Church; others to bring them into the Church; some because they are "federally holy;" others "to wash away the guilt of original sin;" others, perhaps, as Mr. C. W. Miller, because (as quoted by Dr. Bledsoe*):

"*Little children occupy precisely the relation to Jesus Christ, which a regenerated, justified, sanctified adult sustains*"!!

Were this difficulty settled among themselves, it would relieve the defenders of the dogma of a very heavy incubus. The suggestion made by Dr. Pendleton is a good one. For their special benefit it is here repeated:

"It would be well for the various tribes of Pedobaptists to call a general council and try and decide why infants should be baptized. The reasons in favor of the practice

---

Southern Review for July, 1874, p. 181.

are, at present, so contradictory and so destructive of one another that it must involve the advocates of the system in great perplexity. Many, though, would object to such a council, because, for obvious reasons, the Pope of Rome should preside over it, and others would object because it would probably be in session as long as the Council of Trent. Still, if one good reason could be furnished for infant baptism, by the combined wisdom of Catholics and Protestants, it would be more satisfactory than all the reasons which are now urged."

But *is* the Church of Christ the same as the Jewish Church? Even the most rigid Pedobaptists will not give an unqualified affirmative to this simple question. Hence the appearance in their writings of such expressions as the following: "*Substantial* oneness;" "The same in *substance;*" and even Dr. Rice, after making the bold statement as given above, speaks of the "chief and only important *difference* between the two dispensations." Receive *in toto* the sameness of the churches, and if consistent, you must go even beyond Roman Catholicism. No one would surely have the temerity to deny that there are *great changes, and differences* between the two churches. Then it must be shown clearly and unequivocally that these *changes* and *differences* did not, *in the least*, affect *the conditions of membership;* or, in other words, that ALL who were in, or were entitled to membership in, the Jewish Church, are in, or are entitled to membership in, the Church of Christ; and that, too, *upon precisely the same terms.* Until this be done the identity theory avails nothing to infant baptism. To do this is a herculean task.

"Not even the eloquence of Dr. Hodge can make it seem probable that the Jewish nation was an exact model of the Christian Church in respect to membership, when in almost every other respect it was unlike that church."

Admitting, and you must admit, that there were *some* changes made in the character of members, and also in the terms of membership, then how are we to know who are to be received into Christ's Church, and allowed to partake of its ordinances, and what the terms of membership now? Or, in other words, to what extent do these admitted differences affect the terms of membership in *this continued church?* The *New Testament* is our only guide. The argument *reductio ad absurdum* has shown, in the preceding chapter, that it will not do to accept that which is not *forbidden* in the New Testament. Only that must be received which is *positively commanded*. The golden and the only safe rule is to OBEY CHRIST—"to do *nothing* either *more* or *less* or *different* from what he has told us." But from the New Testament, where Christ's commands are recorded, nothing can be learned about either the baptism of infants or their membership in *his* church. For, as Dr. Bledsoe says:

"With all our searching we have been unable to find in the New Testament a single express declaration or word in favor of infant baptism;" and "hundreds of learned Pedobaptists have come to the same conclusion; *especially* since the New Testament has been subjected to a closer, more conscientious, and more candid exegesis than was formerly practiced."

Granting, therefore, for argument sake, that the

churches are the same, it by no means follows that *infants* are in the church, or should be baptized. *But are the churches one?* Let the candid reader, seeking above all things to know *the truth,* consider the *following facts,* and say whether there exists that "*identity*" claimed by Pedobaptists. *First; If the two churches are the same, then all the Jews, as well as all who had been proselyted to the Jewish religion and brought into the Jewish Church, were members of the Church of Christ while he was on earth.* This statement you must accept as true, or reject the "identity theory." Just think of it. Those who were Christ's most inveterate enemies while on earth, and against whom he aimed his heaviest and severest blows, were the Lawyers, the Scribes, the Sadducees, and Pharisees; and yet upon this hypothesis all of these same parties were prominent members in his church. There are many portions of Scripture that might be read just here with great profit. Turn to Matthew xxiii. 13–39. Listen to the keen, pealing words of the Master, his very soul blazing with righteous indignation. Think you that those of whom he spoke were members of *his* church? What epithets he uses—"hypocrites," "blind guides," "fools," as "whited sepulchers," "serpents," "generation of vipers," "children of hell"—the strongest denunciatory words ever used by the Son of God! And yet, the "identity theory" makes *these* persons members of the Christian Church. "Woe unto you Scribes and Pharisees, hypocrites! for ye are like whited sepulchers, which indeed appear beautiful outward, but are within full of dead men's bones, and of all uncleanliness. Even so ye outwardly appear righteous unto men, but within ye are full of hypocrisy and iniquity." The Savior charged them with "the blood of the prophets," and "with all the righteous blood shed upon the earth." "Ye serpents, ye generation of vipers, how can ye escape the damnation of hell?" Yet all these were members in good standing in the Church of Christ, if it was identical with the Jewish Church! How monstrously absurd! And if character will not exclude them, surely the words of the Master will: "Woe unto you, Scribes and Pharisees, hypocrites! for ye shut up the kingdom of heaven against men: for ye *neither go in yourselves*, neither suffer ye them that are entering to go in." Pedobaptists tell us that by "kingdom of heaven" is meant the "visible Church" of Christ, which is the "*same*" as "the Jewish Church." But it is clear that these parties who "shut up the kingdom of heaven," were *in the Jewish Church* and *outside of* "the kingdom of heaven" (or, as it is called "the visible church"), "for ye neither *go in yourselves*," etc. The Church of Christ, which they would not enter, and the Jewish Church of which they were members, can not therefore be the same church—unless perchance a person can be both *in* and *out* of the same thing at the same time. And those persons who were *entering* were Jews, and therefore members of the Jewish Church already, and therefore could not be *entering* the Jewish Church. They were *in the* Jewish Church, but being *out of*, were *entering* the Church of Christ. How could persons *in* the Jewish Church be entering the same church? Pedobaptists may reconcile these difficulties. Their system is full of contradictions.

But hear further the scathing words of Him who spake as never man spake: " Woe unto you, Scribes and Pharisees, hypocrites! for ye compass sea and land to make one proselyte " (*i. e.*, bring a man into the Jewish Church); " and when he is made " (or brought in) " ye make him twofold more the child of hell than yourselves." What! a person a member in Christ's Church and a " child of hell "! A person brought into the Church of Christ made " twofold more a child of hell," than those already members! Yes; if the Church of Christ is the same as the Jewish Church! Oh, shade of Aristotle, whither hast thou gone? These are not absurdities, but verities, if the " identity theory " be true. As, therefore, *these* must be accepted, or *it* rejected, Pedobaptists prefer to do the former, startling as it is; but Baptists, the latter. They will not, they can not, accede to any theory that drives to such monstrous and hideous absurdities. Were *the Jews members of the Church of Christ?* Then *his church* cried, Away with him, away with him; crucify him; let his blood be upon us and our children; nay, do not release unto us *our head,* our king, but let him die, and release Barabbas, the robber and the murderer.

Moreover, Paul was a respectable member of the Jewish Church, yet he persecuted and made "havoc" of the Church of Christ. Was he a member of the church he was persecuting, and against which his whole soul burned with furious rage? Did he, from the influence of that Damascus vision, and from the change wrought in him by the Holy Spirit, make no change in his *church relations?* The question needs no answer.

And on the day of Pentecost, that grandest of all days in the history of Christ's Church, three thousand souls, all of whom were Jews, "*were added*" unto his *church.* How could these persons, *already* members in the *Jewish Church,* be *added* to his church—if it was the same? "And the Lord *added* to *the church* daily such as should be saved," or those who are saved. But these additions were made not to the *Jewish Church,* but to the *Church of Christ.* Many Jews, even many of the priests, became obedient to the faith, and were put out of the Jewish Church for going into the Church of Christ. It is impossible for them to be the same.

This theory, moreover, would force us to another absurdity, viz: If it be true, then all the Jews of to-day are members of the Church of Christ. Recall the syllogism just given, and with a slight change the fallacy of the argument is very manifest. Thus: The Christian Church is the same as the Jewish Church; but (instead of infants, write) all the Jews, Scribes, Pharisees, and Sadducees, as well as all the proselytes to their religion, were members of the Jewish Church; therefore, all the Jews, the Scribes, the Pharisees, the Sadducees, as well as all the proselytes to their religion, were members of the Christian Church. Pedobaptists may have the argument for what it is worth. Its weakness will certainly appear to the most careless reader of these pages.

AGAIN: *Both Jews and Gentiles were received into the Church of Christ upon precisely the same terms.*

Into his kingdom and into his church they both must *enter*. Neither were in it by virtue of their birthright. This fact is worthy of great emphasis. Descent from Abraham entitled no one to membership in, and the immunities of, the Church of the Lord Jesus Christ. "Think not to say within yourselves, we have Abraham to our father,"* etc. As little, to-day does our ancestry, however beloved and honored, give a passport to church-membership, to its ordinances, or to the joys of heaven. As the Jews were born into the Jewish Commonwealth, so both Jew and Gentile in the kingdom of Christ, are "born, not of blood, nor of the will of the flesh, nor of the will of man, but of God."† Even to Nicodemus, a distinguished Jewish Rabbi, a member of their highest court, Christ said:‡ "Marvel not that I said unto *thee* [Jewish Rabbi as thou art], ye [Jews, even you who are members of the Sanhedrim, the highest of your nation] *must*

---
*Matthew iii. 9.
†John i. 13.
‡John iii. 7

be born again." That you are Abraham's children will not avail, for all " that which is born of the flesh is flesh, and [only] that which is born of the Spirit is spirit." That you have observed all the forms and ceremonies of the temple worship, according to the demands of Judaism; that you were " circumcised the eighth day, of the stock of Israel, of the tribe of Benjamin, a Hebrew of the Hebrews, as touching the law a Pharisee;" still all this does not avail. For the Jews stood before God on the same footing with the Gentiles who " were without Christ, being aliens from the commonwealth of Israel, and strangers from the covenants of promise, having no hope, and without God in the world." " Neither circumcision availeth anything, nor uncircumcision, but a new creature." And " now in Christ Jesus (both the Jew and the Gentile), who sometime were far off are made nigh by the blood of Christ." And " there is no difference between the Jew and the Greek: for the same Lord over all is rich unto all that call upon him."* In the New Birth, as to its necessities as well as to its blessings, there is no distinction of nationalities. With respect to *that* especially, " there is neither Greek nor Jew, circumcision nor uncircumcision, Barbarian, Scythian, bond nor free: but Christ is all, and in all."† And in *this* " there is neither Jew nor Greek, their is neither bond nor free, there is neither male nor female: for ye are all *one* in Christ Jesus."‡ " Ye must be born again "

---
*Romans x. 12.
†Colossians iii. 11.
‡Galatians iii. 28.

is a *universal* necessity. For " except a man [*i. e.*, any one] be born from above, he can not see the kingdom of God."* The same gospel is preached to all. Hence Paul preached, " testifying both to the *Jews*, and also to the *Greeks*, repentance toward God and faith toward our Lord Jesus Christ."† If, then, it be true, and certainly none will deny it, that the *Jew* as well as the Gentile, had to *enter* the Church of Christ, and that they both *entered on precisely the same terms*, does it not follow, conclusively, that his church was a body entirely different from and independent of the Jewish Church? Else the Jew would have been a member in the Church of Christ, by virtue of his being a Jew, and could not have been *added to it*, as the Scripture says he was. These are only a few of the *facts* which are at war with the " identity theory," and which no mortal man can ever harmonize with it.

" Is the Christian Church that rejected the great body of the Jewish nation, the same with the Jewish Church, which by God's appointment contained the whole nation? Was the church into which its members were born, the same with the church whose members must be born from above—born not of blood, nor of the will of the flesh, nor of the will of man, but of God? Was the church that admitted every stranger to its passover, without any condition of faith or character, merely complying with a certain regulation that gave circumcision to their males, without any condition of

---
*John iii. 3.
†Acts xx. 21.

faith or character, the same with the church which requires faith and true holiness in all who enjoy its ordinances? Was the church that contained the Scribes and Pharisees, and Sadducees, the most cruel, determined, open and malignant enemies of Christ—the same with that church into which such persons could not enter without a spiritual birth?" There is but one answer to be given to all these questions. And that will be given by every intelligent, unbiased person. It is, No.

FINALLY; Christ made out of *twain*—the Jews and the Gentiles—*one new man, i. e., one new body* or church.* And that *new* church was his church, composed of and open to the *twain*—both Gentiles and Jews, and in no sense one with the Jewish Church. "For by one Spirit are we all baptized into *one body*, whether we be Jews or Gentiles, whether we be bond or free; and have been all made to drink into one Spirit."† There is no such thing as the identity of the churches. And further, only for the sake of argument has the Jewish Church been spoken of as a reality. But there is no such thing. There was the "Commonwealth of Israel," the Jewish Theocracy, or the Jewish nation, as there was a Gentile nation out of both which (of the twain) Christ obtained the materials to make his *new church*. But this was no such thing as a church in the true sense of the term. And never was there such a thing as a *church* un-

---
*Ephesians ii. 15.
†1 Corinthians xii. 13.

til Christ established his. Away then goes the argument founded upon church identity. And with it goes one of the strongest pillars of Pedobaptism—its most colossal shaft is broken. It is useless to urge this as an argument for infant membership or infant baptism.

"And yet upon this identity Mr. Hibbard says, 'we rest the weight of the *whole argument* for infant baptism.' It rests upon a foundation of sand. Mr. H. is in a dilemma. He may choose either horn of the dilemma and it will gore him unmercifully. If such a foundation can sustain the argument for infant baptism, there is no *weight* in the argument; but if the weight of the argument crushes the foundation, there is no *solidity* in the foundation."

CHAPTER VIII.

CLOSELY allied with the subject discussed in the last chapter, and, in fact, depending upon that for whatever of strength it may have, is the question of "*Baptism in the room of circumcision.*" And all the arguments made to bear against the "identity theory," can be pressed with equal strength against this question. As has been seen, Pedobaptists give very different and conflicting reasons for admitting infants to the ordinance of Christian baptism. In fact, Dr. Bushnell, one of them, does not hesitate to affirm that * " No *settled* opinions of the *grounds* and *import* of infant baptism have ever been attained to" by them all.

In his *Life of Christ*† Dr. Hanna, says:

"Why, then, do we baptize *infants?* No express mention is made of infants in the command of Christ which instituted this rite (of baptism); no distinct case of the baptism of infants is mentioned in the sacred narratives. Are we not acting, then, without a divine warrant? are we not contradicting the inherent nature and design of this ordinance when infants are baptized by us? If it be true, as we are distinctly taught it is, that in the spiritual commonwealth of the church, baptism takes that place which in the Jewish commonwealth was occupied by cir-

---

*Howell's "Evils of Infant Baptism," p. 90.
†Vol. III. p. 310.

cumcision, each being the initiatory or admission rite of the society, then it will at once appear that there is scarcely an objection to the *baptism* of infants, which might not with equal weight be urged against the *circumcision* of infants."

There are several things in this quotation to be noticed. And first, all that the Doctor had written on the nature and design of baptism, preceding this quotation, could be presented as an argument against baptizing unintelligent infants. Hence his question—"Why *then?*" etc., as if he felt the necessity of reconciling that practice with the *design* of the ordinance. He makes no attempt to do that. For such an attempt would be useless. The silence of the New Testament on the subject is also unreservedly conceded—that neither in the *command* of Christ which *instituted* baptism, nor in the sacred narratives, which give an account of the baptisms administered by the apostles, is there anything said about *infants* or *infant baptism*. That is unaccountable if the practice be of *divine appointment* and not of men. And the question is very pertinent: "Are we not, then [in view of this fact], acting without divine warrant? Are we not contradicting the inherent nature and design of this ordinance [as he himself had just before given it] when infants are baptized by us?" Most unquestionably you are, if God has said nothing about it, as is confessed over and over again.

Nor does he agree with many of his distinguished brethren that infants are baptized because they are already in the church, but rather they come in by baptism as the initiatory (?) rite. Resting the whole theory on the simple supposition that baptism has taken the place of the rite of circumcision, the Doctor, feeling that this is his only refuge (nor does he feel very secure and confident in it), says: "There is scarcely an objection to the *baptism* of infants, which might not with equal weight be urged against the *circumcision* of infants." What if that be true; or even more than that, and he had said not a *single* objection? Would that have proved any thing in favor of infant baptism? Would that fact have been conclusive that the rite was of divine appointment? Would that have atoned for the silence of the New Testament on the subject? Is the difficulty,—that Christ said nothing about it, although he instituted the ordinance of baptism, and that the apostles said nothing about it, although laboring under his command,—swept away by the simple announcement that all the objections urged against this dogma can be urged against the rite of circumcision? Is it not a marvel that *any one*, to say nothing of Dr. Hanna, should have thought so?

But there is *one serious objection,* at least, which can be made against the one but not against the other, viz: *The one* is authorized by a *plain, positive command* from the God of heaven, while about *the other* there is not a single word in all the oracles of God. The one is of divine appointment, the other is not. God commanded to circumcise the child, but *where* has he commanded its baptism? If he has done so, is it not strange that all the Pedobaptists in the world have never found it? And when one declares he has found a command to baptize infants, all the rest laugh him to scorn, so preposterous is his claim! Give the same reason for baptizing as the Jews did for circumcising the infant, viz, a *positive command from God*, and the controversy is at an end.

But let it be asked again why this frightful abandoning of the New Testament? We *must* abide the decisions of *that book*. And it is here reasserted, therefore, with great emphasis, that BY THE NEW TESTAMENT INFANT BAPTISM MUST STAND OR FALL. "If baptism was ordained by Jesus Christ, we should allow him to decide who are to be baptized, and not refer the matter to either Abraham or Moses. . . . . Was there ever such a course adopted before to establish a divine ordinance? Ask a Jew why his ancestors for so many centuries observed the feasts of the Passover, Pentecost and the Tabernacles, and he will tell you that God commanded them to do so. Ask a Christian why believers should be baptized and partake of the Lord's Supper? And his response will be, these are injunctions of Jesus Christ. Ask a Pedobaptist, however, why infants ought to be baptized? And he will at once plunge into the mazes of Judaism . . . . insisting most strenuously on the substitution of baptism for circumcision." This is a strange method of proving that infants ought to be baptized. Give a *command* for it—JUST ONE— and then argument is not needed. The argument, which is generally constructed by Pedobaptists upon this assumption in support of their "theory — a huge inverted pyramid resting upon a single point, and that point a mere assumption, and one in itself unwarrantable and unreasonable"—may also be stated in a syllogism about as follows: Baptism has come in the room of circumcision. But infants were circumcised. Therefore, infants must be baptized. This does not appear very conclusive. In fact it has been abandoned by many very able Pedobaptist divines. And this further justifies a remark already made, viz: that every argument ever advanced in favor of infant baptism has at some time been abandoned even by the defenders of the rite.

In the Baptist edition of his work on Baptism,* Moses Stuart says:

" How unwary, too, are many excellent men in contending for infant baptism, on the ground of the Jewish analogy of circumcision. The covenant of circumcision furnishes *no grounds* for infant baptism."

Some three years ago, or thereabouts, the following statement was published in the *Religious Herald*, as coming from Henry Ward Beecher:

" I concede and I assert, first, that infant baptism is no where commanded in the New Testament. Secondly, I affirm that the cases where it is implied, as the baptism of whole households, are by no means conclusive and without doubt, and if there is no other basis for it than that, it is not safe to found it on the practice of the apostles in the baptism of Christian families. Therefore, l give up what has been injudiciously used as an argument for infant baptism. And, thirdly, I assert that the doctrine that as a Christian ordinance it is a substitute for the circumcision of the Jews, *is a doctrine utterly untenable.*"

---

*The Introductory Review, p. 32.

Surely, there must be a very manifest weakness in an argument that fails to convince those most anxious to be convinced, and that, too, men* who are capable of testing an argument.

But, beyond all this, it is wholly gratuitous to assume, as is done in this argument, that baptism is a substitute for circumcision. The Scriptures do not so teach. Their silence upon this is only equaled by their silence concerning infants being the subjects of Christian baptism. The facts of the Scriptures are contrary to any such assumption. In the old dispensation there were figures and types of Christ and his church, which were fulfilled in the new dispensation. And the separate parts of the Church of Christ may find counterparts there. Circumcision *was a type*. But it could not be the type of baptism, *for baptism is also a type.* Who ever heard of one type being the type of another type? Can a shadow cast a shadow? For every shadow—as for both baptism and circumcision—there must be a corresponding *substance*.

Circumcision is the type, not of baptism, *which is also a type*, but of *regeneration;* this is the circumcision not made with hands. Regeneration, or the New Birth, is the substance; circumcision is the shadow. The rules in Hermeneutics, by which these things are regulated, are very simple and explicit. The following is recognized by all as sound: "No *external* institution or fact in the Old Testament is a type of an *external* institution or

---

*Whatever be your opinion of Mr. Beecher, you can not deny his ability to examine and weigh an argument.

fact in the New Testament. *External* institutions or facts in the Old Testament are *invariably* types of *internal* and *spiritual* institutions and facts in the New Testament." How in the world, then, could circumcision, an *external institution* of the Old Testament, be a type of baptism, an *external institution* of the New Testament! *It is not.* It is, however, a type of the *internal, spiritual* work wrought in the heart by the Holy Spirit in the New Birth. This is the circumcision of the heart. With this agrees Turrettine,* the successor of the great John Calvin. He says:

"But one type can not be shadowed forth by another type," since "both are brought forward to represent one truth. So circumcision shadowed forth *not baptism*, but the grace of regeneration; and the passover represented not the Lord's Supper, but Christ set forth in the Supper."

The regenerated have the circumcision of the heart, of which that in the flesh was a type. "In whom (Christ) also ye are circumcised with the circumcision made without hands, in putting off the body of the sins of the flesh by the circumcision of (made by) Christ."† "For he is not a Jew, which is one *outwardly;* neither is that circumcision, which is outward in the flesh: But he is a Jew, which is one inwardly; and circumcision is that of the heart, in the spirit, and not in the letter; whose praise is not of men, but of God.‡"

And again. Judaism has ever been a most hos-

---
*Howell's Evils of Infant Baptism, p. 78.
†Colossians ii. 11.
‡Romans ii. 28, 29.

tile enemy to Christianity. And the many Jewish converts, in the early churches, labored most strenuously to append to the simplicity of the gospel some of their old customs, and especially the rite of circumcision. And these Judaizing teachers troubled the churches not a little with their teaching—their talking about circumcision. And consequently the Gentile Christians became dissatisfied, and complained that they did not enjoy equal privileges with the Jews, in not being circumcised.

This could easily have been settled, had the apostle just reminded them, as the Pedobaptists would do, that baptism had come in the room of circumcision; that their baptism was the same as, and therefore equal to, the circumcision of the Jew, and not a whit, therefore, were they behind the Jewish converts. But they would have at once responded, yes; but the Jews have *both*—they have been baptized as well as circumcised, while we have only been baptized.

But as circumcision was not substituted by baptism, the apostle could not, and therefore did not, respond in this supposed way. But he told the Gentile converts plainly, that *they had a circumcision*—one that was higher than that of the Jew, as the substance is more than the shadow; even the circumcision *of the heart,* in Christ, one not made with hands. "In Christ *ye were also* circumcised with a circumcision not made with hands."*" "Circumcision is that of the *heart,* in *the Spirit*"

---

*Bible Union Translation of Colossians ii. 11.

"Stand fast therefore in the liberty wherewith Christ hath made us free, *and be not entangled again with the yoke of bondage.* Behold, I Paul say unto you, that if ye be circumcised, Christ shall profit you nothing. For I testify again to every man that is circumcised, that he is a debtor to do the whole law."* " For we are the circumcision [*i. e.,* Jews, individually, who enjoy, not the circumcision which is outward in the flesh, but the circumcision of the heart, in the spirit,] who worship God in the spirit, and rejoice in Christ Jesus, and have no confidence in the flesh."† " As many as desire to make a fair show in the flesh, they constrain you to be circumcised; only lest they should suffer persecution for the cross of Christ. For neither they themselves who are circumcised keep the law; but desire to have you circumcised, that they may glory in your flesh. But God forbid that I should glory, save in the cross of our Lord Jesus Christ, by whom the world is crucified unto me, and I unto the world. For in Christ Jesus neither circumcision [that in the flesh] availeth anything, nor uncircumcision, *but a new creature.*"‡ " If any man be in Christ, *he is a new creature:* old things are passed away; behold, all things are become new."§ " For in Jesus Christ neither circumcision availeth any thing, nor uncircumcision; but faith which worketh by love." ‖ Such were the statements made by an inspired writer to satisfy those

---

*Galatians v. 1–3. †Philippians iii. 3. ‡Galatians vi. 12–15.
§2 Corinthians v. 17. ‖Galatians v. 6.

troubled Gentile converts, that they were equally blessed with the Jews, those of the circumcision. And not once does he intimate that their baptism took the place of the circumcision of the Jew.

And, moreover, when this same question about circumcision was agitating the church at Antioch, the whole matter was referred to the apostles at Jerusalem. And there before the apostles, the elders, and the *whole multitude* of believers, it was *fully discussed and settled*, and not one word said, so far as the record goes, about baptism having come in the place of circumcision. And then " it pleased *the apostles, and elders, with the whole church*, to send chosen men of their own number to Antioch." And by these chosen men a letter was sent to the church at that place. But in *this letter** there is not the slightest intimation that baptism had taken the place of circumcision. This is significant. Here is a letter written by inspired men, for the express purpose of settling a difficulty which had arisen in a church, about whether the Gentile converts must be circumcised, as the law directed concerning the Jew in the old dispensation, and yet nothing is said about baptism. The whole difficulty could have been disposed of by the simple announcement that baptism had come in the room of circumcision, and therefore the latter was not to be practiced. If this Pedobaptist notion were true, verily here is a call for its statement. But these men, although acting under the guidance of

---
* Acts xv. 23–29.

the Holy Spirit, said not one word about it, and, so far as we know, thought of no such thing.

Another fact from Scripture, which antagonizes the idea of baptism taking the place of the Jewish rite, is: In the apostolic days, persons who had received the rite of circumcision, afterward, upon becoming disciples, were baptized also. It was so with those (the male part of them) whom John baptized. Even the Savior himself was circumcised and *afterward baptized* by John.* So also were the disciples he made and baptized, for he made his disciples from among the Jews. A large number of the devout men, converted on the day of Pentecost, had no doubt previously been circumcised, and yet when they "had gladly received the word," they were baptized. Paul was both circumcised and baptized.† And what, if possible, is stranger still, if this theory be true, is, Paul circumcised Timothy‡ even after he had become a disciple, and *therefore after he had been baptized*. How could baptism be administered in the place of circumcision, when the latter is still indifferently practiced?

These facts are irreconcilable, with the supposition that baptism has taken the place of circumcision.

But, further, *the facts of Pedobaptism, as now practiced by no means correspond with the facts of Jewish circumcision*. Admitting, for argument sake, their theory to be true, then the *law of cir-*

---

* Luke ii. 21. Matt. iii. 13.
† Phil. iii. 5. Acts ix. 18.
‡ Acts xvi. 3.

cumcision must decide who are to be baptized—of what *age*, also of what *sex* the person shall be. *This law* is given in Genesis xvii.

1. It requires, and such was the practice among the Jews, that only the *males* be circumcised. Not only males, but *females* also, are baptized. If baptism take the place of circumcision, then by that law it must be limited to *male* children and *male* adults.

2. Circumcision, by positive law, was to be administered to only the male children, and that, too, on the *eighth day after* their birth. Do Pedobaptists follow this rule? No; but contrariwise, they baptize (but by what law no one knows) both male and *female*, children at *any age*, from birth up *to thirteen years* (the writer never heard of a person older than this, who was baptized upon the plea of infant (?) baptism).

Let Pedobaptists know that they are to sprinkle their children on the eighth day after their birth—not sooner or later—and that they are to sprinkle only the *male* and not the *female* portion.

3. Circumcision, by positive law from God, extended to all the *male servants* in the house of the Jew, even "those bought with their money." Do Pedobaptists follow this rule in their practice? Manifestly not. To be consistent with this theory, a master when converted and baptized, should immediately baptize, not only his *male* children, but also his *male servants*, without regard to age or character. Short of these he could not stop, beyond

them he could not go, by the law of circumcision.

Those born in his house must be baptized on the *eighth day* after birth, and those bought with his money he must also baptize, though threescore and ten years old, and that, too, by virtue of the master's baptism!

4. Any one was allowed to perform the rite of circumcision, but Pedobaptists (most of them) require that a regular ordained minister shall administer the ordinance of Christian baptism, even to an infant.

If there is a man in the United States who would develop and present in its full strength whatever argument there might be in this theory, that man is Dr. Nathan L. Rice, of the Presbyterian Church. He has spent his full strength on it, and has put it before the world in syllogistic form; and this has been repeated throughout the length and breadth of the land as the *unanswerable argument for infant baptism*. If it be swept away, the whole argument is gone that can be drawn from the theory of the covenants. The syllogism of the Doctor appeared in the *Presbyterian Expositor*,* published in Chicago, and he thus expresses his own confidence in this master effort of his to defend the cause:

"We will state the argument from the Abrahamic covenant, and we defy any one to admit the position without

---

* Vol. II. pp. 16, 17. This quotation was obtained from a minister of this State, who took it from the original work when first published.

admitting the doctrine of infant baptism as a logical necessity."

This argument will be stated in full; but, by the use of brackets, will be inserted what every one will recognize as *scriptural facts*. This can not be objected to, and the fallacy of the argument will be manifested at once by the insertion.

"1. The covenant with Abraham is the covenant of grace, therefore it did not belong to the Jewish dispensation and did not pass away with it.

"2. The covenant confessedly embraced believers and their infant children [(*i. e.*) *male* believers and their *male children, infants,* boys and men, together with all their servants, whether born in their house or bought with their money, infants, boys and men] and since it remains unchanged it embraces THEM still.

"3. All who were in the covenant had a right to its seal, and those now embraced in it have the same right. And since professed believers and their infant children [*male children*, infants, boys and men; *male servants*, infants, boys and men —Genesis xvii. 23-27] did receive the seal of the covenant by express command of God, the *same characters* [male believers and their male children, infants, boys and men; all the male servants and their male children, infants, boys and men] must receive it still.

"4. As circumcision was the first seal, and was administered to professed believers and their infant children [(*i. e*) *male* believers and their infant children, *male* infants, boys and men; with all the male servants, whether bought with money or born in their house, and their male children], so *baptism is now the seal and must be administered to the* SAME CHARACTERS [but certainly to no others, by the *law of* circumcision].

"Here we might stop," continues the Doctor, (so he might) "but we will give the argument in another form, thus:

"1. The Abrahamic covenant was and is the covenant of grace; and the Church of God, as a people in covenant with him, was organized on this covenant.

"2. As the Church was organized on this covenant, it embraced in its membership all who were embraced in the covenant, viz: professed believers and their infant children [(*i. e.*) male believers and their *male* children, infants, boys and men; all the male servants, and their *male children*, infants, boys and men—these constituted the membership and no others].

"3. The Christian Church stands on the same covenant and is identical with the Abrahamic Church, and embraces THE SAME CHARACTERS in its membership, viz: professed believers and their infant children [(*i. e.*) *male* believers and their male children, infants, boys and men, etc.].

"4. All embraced in the covenant and in the church-membership are entitled to the initiatory rite; and since professed believers and their infant children [(*i. e.*) *male* believers and their *male children*, infants, boys and men; all the *male servants* and their *male children* also, infants, boys and men and *no others certainly*] did receive circumcision, the first initiatory rite, the SAME CHARACTERS, [and NO OTHERS by this law] being still embraced in the same covenant and in the same Church, have a right to baptism, which is now the initiatory rite.' (The emphasis on the Doctor's words is mine.)

What do *you* think of this argument? Is it conclusive? Granting the premises, which has been done for the sake of argument, and what is proved? Simply this, that *male believers* and their *male children*, infants, boys and men; and all the *male servants* and their male children, infants, and boys and men, are all in the Church and are entitled to baptism! Do *you* accept the conclusion? The difficulty with the argument is, the premises do not contain all the *scriptural facts* on the subject; and a false conclusion is therefore a "logical necessity." Supply these facts, as has been done, and the argument vanishes like dew before the morning sun. It is impossible to learn who are to be baptized, *by the law of circumcision;* and we are forced back to the New Testament. But there not one word is found about infant baptism; simply that of believers or disciples is mentioned, and commanded, and practiced. Until Pedobaptists are willing to take the substitution theory IN TOTO, they should remain silent in reference to it. If baptism comes in the room of circumcision, then it must be practiced *according to the law of circumcision; you must neither stop short of that law nor go beyond it;* but simply baptize such persons, at such ages, as were circumcised—no more, no less. Where is the man who will do this? By what authority is one part accepted, another part dropped off, a third part added on, just as perchance it may suit the fancy? Is not such havoc made of the word of God, a dangerous procedure?

Did *Christ command* that baptism be administered to both male *and female* infants, and not to confine it to males, as circumcision was?—that the time for baptizing is not limited to the *eighth day*, as circumcision was, etc., etc.? Where is it recorded? No wonder Moses Stuart, to whom *you* should give audience on this subject, said:

"*Numberless difficulties* present themselves in our way as soon as we begin to argue in such a manner as this"—infant baptism from infant circumcision.

Is it not a manifest weakness of the cause of infant baptism for its advocates to proceed in this way; to abandon the *New Testament* and seek to prove infants to be subjects of a *New Testament ordinance* by *inferences* from the ceremonies of Judaism?

Such a course is scarcely equaled by those Pedobaptist ministers who have said, in defense of their practice, that inasmuch as all of Christ's sayings were not recorded, perhaps the mention of infant baptism was among his unwritten sayings. Perhaps it was!! Just prove it. It is better not to endeavor to be wise above what is written. But once more: *If there be any analogy between the rite of circumcision and the ordinance of Christian baptism, that analogy is utterly subversive of the theory of infant baptism.*

As the one was administered to the *literal seed only*, so the other is administered *only to the spiritual seed* of Abraham, that is, to believers. The *facts* in the case will be briefly stated to justify this statement. The Abrahamic covenant had two phases or aspects; the one a *natural*, the other a *spiritual*. It had also three promises, viz: a numerous posterity; the land of Canaan as a heritage to them; and God would be to him a God, and to his seed after him. Now each of these promises is applicable to, and fulfilled in, both the *natural* and the *spiritual* aspect of the covenant.

1. *The natural* aspect. Here we have the numerous posterity in the hosts of Israel; there was given to them the land of Canaan, flowing with milk and honey; and to them, as Abraham's *natural seed*, Abraham's God was their God.

2. The spiritual aspect. There is here also a *numerous posterity*. All believers in the Lord Jesus Christ are the *spiritual seed* of Abraham. Hence he is called "the father of the faithful (*i. e.*), of the believing. "Know ye therefore that they which are of faith [*i. e.*, believers], *the same are the children of Abraham.*" "So then they which be of faith are blessed with faithful Abraham." "*And if ye be Christ's, then are ye Abraham's seed, and heirs* ACCORDING TO THE PROMISE."* "Therefore it is of faith, that it might be by grace; *to the end the promise might be sure to all the seed;* not to that only which is of the law [the portion who are believing Jews], but to that also [the Gentile portion] which is of the faith of Abraham; who is the father of us all [both Jew and Gentile believers]."† "Not as though the word of God hath taken none effect. For they are not all Israel, which are of Israel: neither, because they are the seed of Abraham, are they all children: but, in Isaac shall thy seed be called. That is, They that are the children of the flesh, these are not the children of God: *but the children of the promise are counted for the seed.*"‡ Who, then, are the *spiritual seed* of Abraham? Manifestly all who are Christ's; who are believers in him: "Even us, whom he hath called, not of the *Jews* only, but also of the *Gentiles;* "§ these are the *spiritual* seed, the children according to promise. And what a numerous posterity, a

---

* Gal. iii. 7, 9, 29.   † Rom. iv. 16.   ‡ Rom. ix. 6-8.
§ Rom. ix. 24.

progeny more numerous than the stars of heaven, or the sand upon the seashore, as God promised Abraham they should be. And also to this *spiritual* seed is promised a Canaan. "They seek a better country, that is an heavenly." Heaven is the promised Canaan to the *spiritual seed* of Abraham. We are travelers and sojourners here in this world, but "heaven is our home"—a land not to be compared with the heritage of natural Israel.

> "There everlasting spring abides,
> And never fading flowers;
> Death, like a narrow stream, divides
> That heavenly land from ours.
>
> "Sweet fields, beyond the swelling flood,
> Stand dressed in living green;
> So to the Jews fair Canaan stood,
> While Jordan rol ed between."

"For this cause I bow my knees unto the Father of our Lord Jesus Christ, of whom the *whole family in heaven and earth* is named."

> "*One family* we dwell in him;
> *One Church* above, beneath;
> Though now divided by the stream,
> The narrow stream of death.
>
> "*One Army* of the living God,
> To his command we bow;
> Part of the host have crossed the flood,
> And part are crossing now.

And surely in a pre-eminent degree the God of Abraham, of Isaac and of Jacob, is the God of Abraham's *spiritual seed* after him. "One God over all, blessed forevermore."

The above is but a brief statement of *acknowledged facts*, and now their application to the subject in hand is simple and easy.

If baptism has come in the place of circumcision, which applied to Abraham's *natural* seed as a national mark, then analogy demands that baptism be *confined* to his natural seed, and therefore only Jews would be entitled to the ordinance.

But the *natural aspect* has all passed away, and now the *spiritual alone* remains. And if baptism comes in the room of circumcision, to whom, according to analogy, must it be administered? Most certainly to all of Abraham's *spiritual seed*, and to them *exclusively*. And these are no others than those who are Christ's, (*i. e.*) believers in him; these are the *spiritual seed* of Abraham, and heirs, according to the promise. Nothing avails now but "faith that worketh by love." "We are all the children of God by faith in Christ Jesus." By this analogy baptism *must be* administered to Abraham's *natural* seed or to his *spiritual* seed. Which will you take? The former? Then you can baptize Jews only, and if you persist in baptizing infants too, you must confine your work to *Jewish* infants, as his *natural* seed. Do you say the ordinance is confined to his *spiritual* seed—whether Jew or Gentile? Then it is most unquestionably limited to believers or disciples, for no others are his spiritual seed. In either case, therefore, the baptism of, at least, Gentile children is out of the question. And so even by this none but believers are entitled to or are the subjects of Christian baptism. This is the conclusion reached from every starting point. For this reason Dr. Hodge, that giant among Pedobaptists, wrote as follows :*

"When Christ came the commonwealth was abolished, and there was nothing put in its place. The Church remained * * * *a spiritual society* with *spiritual promises*, on the condition of *faith in Christ*. In no part of the New Testament is any other condition of membership in the Church presented, than that contained in the answer of Philip to the eunuch, who desired baptism : 'If thou believest with all thy heart, thou mayest. And he answered and said, I believe that Jesus is the Son of God.' The Church, therefore, is in its essential nature *a company of believers*, and not an external society, requiring merely external profession as condition of membership."

Rev. Edward De Pressense, a learned Pedobaptist, of Paris, France, also says :†

"Regarded from the apostolic point of view, baptism can not be connected either with circumcision, or with the baptism administered to proselytes to Judaism. Between it and circumcision there is all the difference which exists between the theocracy to which admission was by birth, and the Church which is entered *only by conversion.*"

Therefore it is concluded that

"Whatever of rational analogy may be traced between circumcision and baptism must inure to the opponents of in-

---

* Quoted in Curtis' Prog. Baptist Prin. p. 92, from *Princeton Review*, Oct., 1853, pp. 684, 685.
† Ford's Christian Repository, Vol. XII. p. 493.

fant baptism. How plain this is! Abraham's *natural* seed were circumcised. * * * Christians are Abraham's spiritual seed. They become so by faith in Christ. * * * It was proper to circumcise Abraham's *natural* seed, it is proper to baptize his *spiritual* seed. But who are his *spiritual* seed? Believers in Christ and believers alone. Infants have no right therefore to baptism, because they are not Abraham's *spiritual seed*. Jewish infants were fit subjects for circumcision, because they were Abraham's *natural* seed. But neither Jewish nor Gentile infants can be *spiritual seed*, because of their incapacity to exercise faith, *and they ought not therefore to be baptized*. I insist, then, that correct analogical reasoning from circumcision to baptism saps the very foundation of Pedobaptism."*

Hence Moses Stuart, as previously quoted, says:

"How unwary, too, are many excellent men, in contending for infant baptism on the ground of the Jewish analogy of circumcision. Are females not proper subjects of baptism? And again, are a man's slaves to be all baptized because he is? Are they church-members of course when they are so baptized? Is there no difference between engrafting into a *politico ecclesiastical* community and into one of which it is said that 'it is not of this world?' In short, numberless difficulties present themselves in our way, as soon as we begin to argue in such a manner as this."

"*The covenant of circumcision furnishes no grounds for infant baptism.*"

And so the Baptists of all ages have said over and over again.

---

* Pendleton's "Three Reasons," p. 56.

CHAPTER IX.

MUCH has already been learned, and much more is yet to be learned from *Church history.* And it opens to the student, on many accounts, a most inviting field. All of its teachings, however, are to be tried most impartially at the bar of Holy Writ —man's only infallible teacher. Concerning what, by divine authority, is binding on man, Church history can teach us nothing, except what is much more plainly taught—and taught with authority too—in the New Testament. Especially is this true touching the ordinances. And with that inspired volume in his hand, therefore, the man, who is utterly ignorant of Church history, can know his *whole duty*, to himself, to his fellow-man, and to his God. For "all Scripture is given by inspiration of God, and is profitable for doctrine, for reproof, for correction, for instruction in righteousness: *That the man of God may be perfect, thoroughly furnished unto all good works.*"* And without that precious volume—precious to all the saints, and lovers of the *"truth as it is in Jesus"* —we are like the mariner, at sea, in a midnight storm, without chart or compass, "tossed to and

---
* 2 Timothy iii. 16, 17.

fro, and carried about with every wind of doctrine." Left to the mercy of merciless winds and a sea as unmerciful, our condition is most pitiable. Oh, who can tell the importance of *clinging* to the *New Testament* as the only compass and chart, that will guide us safely over the sea of uninspired history, beclouded by errors and superstitions of the wildest nature!

And it is altogether proper at this juncture of the investigation, to remind the reader of a fact already learned, viz:

"The historian of infant baptism can gather no materials for his subject from the New Testament. The rite has the sanction of neither precept nor example in the writings of the Evangelists and Apostles. The gloom and the silence of the grave brood over it."

Church history reveals no one fact more plainly than the following: That at a very early period—in the centuries immediately after the apostles—the Church, the doctrines of grace, and *the ordinances* of Christ, were all perverted to a marvelous degree.

And yet amid these superstitious perversions, we are to look for the rise of the doctrine of infant baptism.

Here it had its birth; here it was cradled; and here it grew to manhood. There is an argument (?) used by Pedobaptists called the "*historical* argument for infant baptism." And yet, even they—

"The advocates of infant baptism—find great difficulty in fixing upon the period of its commencement. It is a matter on which great diversity of sentiments exists. They agree only in affirming, that the point of time when the foundations of this system were laid, is to be found somewhere in the long lapse of ages intervening between the call of Abraham out of Ur of the Chaldees, and the third century of the Christian era, when certain Africans were laboring to engraft upon the institutions of the New Testament the wildest vagaries of superstition."

They can agree that "baptism is an ordinance of the New Testament, ordained by Jesus Christ," but are unable to say when and where *infant* baptism had its rise. And on this very fact (the ignorance of the time of its origin) as a foundation, (so hard pressed is their cause) they endeavor to build an argument in its favor! Baseless fabric, indeed! Well, as the *exact time* of its origin may not be certainly known, the next question is, WHEN *is the baptism of infants* FIRST MENTIONED *in history?* Certainly, no one can object if Pedobaptists, who have sought most diligently through all the records of the past, to find something in support of their cause, be allowed to answer this question. The friends of the rite will surely do their best for it.

The six witnesses first introduced are taken from the "*Baptist Short Method.*"* Keep the question before you, and hear the testimony of these *Pedobaptists.*

When is infant baptism first mentioned? Give us the result of your examinations of the annals of history.

Hahn says:

"Neither in the Scriptures, nor during the *first hundred and fifty years*, is a sure example of infant baptism to be found."

---

* Pp. 90-95.

Luther says:

"It can not be proved by the Sacred Scriptures, that infant baptism was instituted by Christ, or begun by the first Christians after the apostles."

Curcellaeus says:

"The baptism of infants in the *two first centuries* after Christ was altogether unknown; but in the *third* and *fourth centuries* was al'owed by some few."

Hyppolytus, Bishop of Pontus, writing in the first half of the *third century*, says:

"We in our days never defended the baptism of children, which in our day had *only begun* to be practiced in some regions."

Bunsen, the learned translator of Hyppolytus, says infant baptism, in the modern sense,

"Was utterly unknown *to the early Church*, not only down to the end of the second century, but indeed to the middle of the *third century*."

Salmasius says:

"In the TWO FIRST centuries no one was baptized, except being instructed in the faith and acquainted with the doctrines of Christ, *he was able to profess himself a believer*."

Neander has written large volumes on Church history; and yet this famous Pedobaptist Church historian, after a most careful study and investigation of the whole matter, deliberately testifies as follows* (is it a falsehood?):

"Baptism was administered at first only to adults, as men were accustomed to conceive baptism and faith as strictly connected. We have ALL REASON [he learned this, in part

---

* Curtis' Prog. Baptist Prin., p. 103.

no doubt, from his investigations of history—in seeing where the rite had its rise] for not deriving infant baptism from apostolic institution." He also says:*

"It is certain that Christ did not ordain *infant* baptism [and yet he ordained the ordinance of Christian baptism.]"†

Mosheim says: ‡

"The sacrament of baptism was administered in this (the first) century, without the public assemblies, in places appointed and prepared for that purpose, and was performed by *an immersion of the whole body in water* in the baptismal *font*. At first it was usual for all who labored in the propagation of the Gospel, to be present at that solemn ceremony; and it was also customary, *that the converts should*

---

* Rice and Campbell Debate, 395.

† While this work was in press the following quotation appeared in the editorial column of *The Religious Herald* (Richmond, Va.), October 28, 1875. And it is here appended to strengthen and to give more at length the testimony of this distinguished man, who, perhaps, has no superior as a Church historian:

"Could any man have found scriptural authority for infant baptism, Neander would have found it. He was a clergyman of the Lutheran Church, in which the rite was practiced. He was a prince among ecclesiastical historians and biblical critics. With all his research and perspicacity, he found no trace of the ceremony in the Scriptures. For convenience, we quote from Benedict's History of the Donatists, pp. 130, 131.

"'Baptism, says he, 'was administered at first only to adults, as men were accustomed to conceive baptism and faith as strictly connected. We have all reason for not deriving infant baptism from apostolical institution, and the recognition of it which followed somewhat later as an apostolical tradition serves to confirm this hypothesis. In the last years of the second century, Tertullian appears as a zealous opponent of infant baptism, a proof that the practice had not yet come to be regarded as an apostolical institution; for, otherwise, he would hardly have ventured to express himself so strongly against it. But if the necessity of infant baptism was acknowledged in theory, it was still far from being uniformly recognized in practice. As the church in North Africa was the first to bring prominently to notice the necessity of infant baptism, so, in connection with this, they also introduced the communion of infants. Church History, Vol. I. pp. 311, 312. Boston Ed.'"

‡ Hist. Maclaine's Translation, pp. 25, 28, 49.

be baptized and received into the church by those under whose ministry they had embraced the Christian doctrine" For "then" he tells us, "Baptism was administered to none but such as had been previously instructed in the principal points of Christianity, and had also given satisfactory proofs of pious dispositions and upright intentions."

And of the *second century* he says:

"The persons that were to be baptized, after they had *repeated the Creed, confessed* and *renounced their sins, and particularly the devil and his pompous allurements, were immersed under water*, and received into Christ's kingdom by a solemn invocation of Father, Son, and Holy Ghost, according to the express command of our Blessed Lord."

Many more might be introduced, who would bear testimony as strongly against infant baptism as the foregoing. But only one more, a Methodist, will be called to testify "when infant baptism was first mentioned in history."

Rev. A. T. Bledsoe, LL.D., assisted by all the light and learning of the *nineteenth* century, in giving the history of this rite, says:*

" Before the time of Tertullian, (A. D. 200) the practice of infant baptism is nowhere distinctly mentioned by any writer of the Church. Those who maintain that it was instituted by the Apostles, and handed down, not by any written word, but only by *oral tradition*, have discovered traces of this practice, *as they imagine*, in the writings of Justin Martyr, and of Irenæus."

The Doctor then shows the groundlessness of any such claim and reiterates:

" Tertullian *is the first writer* in the Church who makes any express mention of the custom of infant baptism. Before his time, *A. D.* 200, *there is not an allusion to the custom from*

---

* *Southern Review* for April, 1874, pp. 336-339.

which its existence may be fairly inferred. It is frequently urged, that the practice of infant baptism must have been an apostolic institution, because it prevailed, and became universal, without the least opposition from any source whatever. But, however strange it may seem, the fact is, that the first father, or writer [Tertullian in the beginning of the third century] by whom the practice is noticed, condemns it as having no foundation either in **reason** or **revelation.**"

Then, if the testimony of Pedobaptists can be relied upon, with a good degree of certainty, it may be stated that the *first* mention *ever* made of infant baptism, was made about the beginning of the *third century*, by Tertullian, who condemned it. (And it may be added that history points strongly to *Africa as the place* of its origin, under the jurisdiction of Cyprian, one of the African pastors.) It was mentioned by no one before Tertullian in the *third century*. Some of the advocates of the practice talk a good deal about certain earlier writers, of Justin Martyr, of Hermas, of Irenæus, and of Polycarp, who, they tell us, was a disciple of John, etc. But if any of these persons anywhere mentioned the practice of baptizing infants, the place has never been found by its most zealous friends. These names are passed over, by the more masterly writers on the subject, such as Dr. Samuel Miller, Dr. Bledsoe, and others, who almost sneer at those who attempt to refer to them as the advocates for the practice. Beyond Tertullian of the third century none of them can go. It is more than *two hundred* years after Christ before infant baptism is *ever mentioned !* It is not easy to stretch the imagination over two hundred years. Our nation is *nearly one* hundred years old—just preparing to celebrate her *one* hundredth anniversary. How many great events have taken place in that time—commencing with that grand struggle in the Revolutionary War for independence, and coming to the present day! All that done inside of *one* hundred years. But it was *twice* that long—*two hundred years*—after Christ before infant baptism was ever mentioned. "Was it from heaven or of men?" *Just think of it.* The *first hundred years* of the Christian era—the most important century in the world's history—*has passed*, and there is not a trace of infant baptism to be found. During this century, Christ came into the world; constituted his Church; offered himself upon the cross as the sacrifice for sin; appointed in his Church the two ordinances—baptism and the Lord's Supper; gave his commission to the disciples, which was to govern them and regulate all their labors to the end of the world; and the disciples, in obedience to that commission, given by their now ascended Lord, go into every nation; preach the gospel and by it make disciples; and then baptize them into the name of the Trinity; gathering these baptized disciples together, they organize them into churches, and teach them to observe all the commandments of Christ. The twelve chosen apostles of our Lord, though some of them lived to a ripe old age, have all died and passed away. The Book of Revelation, the last of the inspired volume, is finished and sealed. And God speaks no more to man except through that finished volume. It contains the whole of his will. The *one hundred years* in which all this is done—the century from which all other centuries date—passes away and *yet not one word is said about the baptism of infants.* The rite is not mentioned once *in all that time.* That is a little singular, to say the least, if it be of divine appointment. Were it of heaven, it *must have been mentioned in that century.*

But further, *another hundred years*—the *second century* of the Christian era—is numbered with the past. And yet *nothing* is said of infant baptism—*not once*, through all those years, *those centuries, is it mentioned.* And this, too, according to the testimony of Pedobaptists themselves. True, in this (the second) century, marked as it was by ignorance, superstitions, and corruptions, the seed of error is sown, which will germinate, and in years yet to come will bring forth the dogma of infant baptism. This *long-continued silence* is one of the loudest and strongest arguments used by Pedobaptists! What a sublime silence of over two hundred years' duration! Who can not hear and understand its awful voice! But the *third century* dawns —if dawning it is, for the dark clouds of ignorance are becoming a deeper black—and the silence is broken. The voice of Tertullian is heard. He is condemning one of the wild superstitions of benighted Africa, viz: the admitting of unintelligent infants to the ordinance of Christian baptism, " as

IS IT FROM HEAVEN OR OF MEN? 145

having no foundation either in reason or revelation." Counting from the ministry of our Savior, *nearly six generations* of people have come into the world and gone out again, and yet, as the advocates of the practice tell us, "there is not an allusion to the custom from which its existence may be fairly inferred." Not one of all that vast multitude, of five generations and over, though by some of these Christ and his apostles were heard, ever heard the mention of this rite. Not one word is to be found in Scripture or early Church history about infant baptism. By the testimony of its friends, infant baptism is not mentioned (and therefore not ordained) by Christ; nor by a single one of his apostles; nor by any one who ever saw an apostle; nor by any one who ever saw any one, who had seen an apostle! And yet it is of divine appointment!!! *Who can believe it?* Do *you?* And do you wonder that Baptists do not, and that they have always fought against it? The New Testament teaches that it is not from heaven; and the first, and inevitable inference is, that it is of men. And this inference is confirmed by Church history.

Pedobaptism is nearly two hundred years younger than the ordinance of Christian baptism. The latter was ordained by Christ, but of the former he said not one word; the latter was practiced by the apostles, but of the former there is not a single trace to be found in all their writings or practice. If infant baptism must be practiced simply because it was practiced sixteen centuries ago, why not do now as was the custom then, viz: *immerse* *the infant?* It was then practiced for the remission of sins; for what it is practiced now, it is very difficult to say. The antiquity of the rite proves not one thing in its favor. An argument from antiquity, to have any weight with Baptists, *with any lover of truth*, must penetrate the gloom and the superstition of the past ages, and extend back into the days of Christ and his apostles, and must be stamped with the unequivocal authority of the New Testament. Such is clearly not the case with infant baptism. Talk not to us, therefore, of the great antiquity of the rite. It is indeed very ancient, but it lacks just *two hundred* years, or more, of being old enough, for its antiquity to amount to anything. And yet Dr. N. L. Rice says:*

"It seems to me impossible that infant baptism could have originated so early, and have become so universal in the Church, unless it is of divine appointment."

Is it possible, that *Dr. Rice* did not see the fallacy of this argument? Who would dare affirm that *whatever* commenced early—even earlier than infant baptism—and prevailed in the Church (of Rome) must therefore be of divine appointment? Will you do it? This *must* be done before the argument can avail. And then you must receive and practice as of divine appointment,

" Many absurd superstitions of the early corrupted Church; such as the worship of images; the invocation of saints; prayers to the Virgin; oblations for the dead; consecration of the baptismal waters; and many others; not a few of which came into use about the time of this; and some of

---

* Ford's Chris. Repos. Vol. XII. p. 408.

which are even older. Not what is *old* but what is *true*, should be our rule; not what *antiquity*, but what the *Bible* teaches, should we obey."

Basil was right in saying:

"It is a manifest mistake in regard to faith, and a clear evidence of pride, either to reject any of those things which the Scripture contains, or to introduce anything that is not written in the sacred pages."

Not *tradition*, but "*the Bible alone* is the religion of Protestants."

By this principle Baptists are willing to stand.

"There are three great principles which Baptists hold, and which they have ever held, with unyielding tenacity, in every period of their history.

"First. THE ALL-SUFFICIENCY AND EXCLUSIVE AUTHORITY OF THE SCRIPTURES AS A RULE OF FAITH AND PRACTICE

"Second. The consequent denial of the right of legislatures and ecclesiastical conventions to impose any rites, ceremonies, observances or interpretations of the Word of God upon our belief and practice.

"Third. The unlimited and unalienable right of every man to expound the Word of God for himself, and to worship God according to the dictates of his own conscience—being responsible in these matters to him only who is King in Zion."*

These principles have made the Baptists, through all the ages, a distinct and a peculiar people. And for these, thousands of Baptists have been numbered with the martyrs of Jesus. These principles have prevented the Baptists from raising their arm against any other people under heaven. For holding to these principles it has been written of them:

"The Baptists are one of the few religious denominations

---

* Dr. Samuel Baker.

that have never persecuted. We can not say that they have been personally too good, seeing that some of them have shown great bitterness toward other religionists, and even toward their own brethren who differed from them; but their immemorial principle of opposition to all union of Church and State has always made it impossible that they should persecute. In so doing they would at once cease to be Baptists." (Dr. John A. Broadus.)

No martyr-blood has ever stained the garments of the Baptists.

The first of these principles was emphasized, both because the others are founded upon it, and also because of its special appositeness here, as showing how Baptists have ever been satisfied with, and would allow no other than, the testimony of the Scriptures on any doctrine or practice. They care not for tradition, or uncertain history, but they *pledge themselves to stand by the Bible and the Bible alone.*

"Can any one tell us," asks Dr. Rice, "in what age infant baptism commenced?" (Baptism, Ch. 5.)

He asserts not.

"Can any one tell us," asks the Roman Bishop of Strasburg, "when the dogma of the real presence in the sacrifice of the mass commenced?" (Letters to the Anglican Clergy.)

He asserts no one can. In what respect does the argument of the Presbyterian Doctor differ from the argument of the Roman Bishop?

"Even if *prelacy* (and why not infant baptism?) were found unequivocally represented as existing by the fathers *in fifty years after the last apostle,* yet, says the great Presbyterian Professor, Dr. Miller, of Princeton, 'If it be not found in the BIBLE, as it assuredly is not, such **testimony** would by no means establish its apostolic appointment. It would only prove that the Church was very early corrupted.'"

What Dr. Miller says about *prelacy* is exactly what Baptists, with precisely the same authority, say about infant baptism. Nothing but a *divine sanction* of *this* rite will be satisfactory to them.

"Can any one tell us when infant baptism commenced?" asks Dr. Rice?

"Can any one tell us," asks Dr. Samuel Miller, (in Christian Ministry) "when the administering of communion to infants was first introduced? By whom? Whether it met with any opposition * * * ? I will venture to say no one can."*

"'Augustine,' says Dr. Knapp, 'calls infant baptism *apostolica traditio;* and we should, unquestionably attach some importance to this testimony, if he had not also called infant communion *apostolica traditio;*' we know he was mistaken in this case. Why not then in the other?"†

The fallacy of the so-called historical argument is certainly manifest to all. Among the very earliest corruptions and superstitions was the perversion of the plan of salvation. And the result was the dogma of baptismal regeneration—or baptism essential to salvation.

And from this sprung the dogma of infant baptism. Bad parentage, surely!

When the Council of Carthage, which was composed of sixty-six Bishops, or Pastors, and over which Cyprian presided, decided in A. D. 253, that the baptism of an infant must not be delayed till

---

* In Ford's Christian Repos. Vol. XII. p. 407.
† Bledsoe in *Southern Review*, April, 1874, p. 344.

the eighth day, the following reason was assigned:

"As far as in us lies, no soul, if possible, is to be lost."*

And Dr. Wall referring to the "Ancient Fathers" says: "They differ concerning the future state of the infant dying unbaptized; but all agreed they missed of heaven."

Salmasius also says:†

"An opinion prevailed that no one could be saved without being baptized; and for that reason the custom arose of baptizing infants."

Infant baptism is easily traced to the dogma of baptismal regeneration. And ever since the one gave birth to the other, the two dogmas have been as closely allied as mother and child. And as the dogma of infant baptism was born of the other; so has it ever received from that, as a child from its mother, nourishment by which it has grown. As Dr. Bledsoe says: (*The Review* for July, 1874, p. 148.)

"The history of infant baptism is, in a very great measure, the history of baptismal regeneration itself. An edition of Shakespeare's 'Hamlet,' with the part of Hamlet omitted, would not be a more ridiculous production than a history of infant baptism without the introduction of baptismal regeneration.

As always so now also,

"There is certainly a logical connection between the doctrine of baptismal regeneration and the practice of administering the saving rite to infants, and even to children yet unborn." (Hovey.)

When saving efficacy had been attributed to bap-

---

* See Pendleton's "Three Reasons," pp. 68, 73.
† Baptist Short Method, p. 98.

tism, then through a desire to save the infant from perdition, the next step would naturally be, to admit the unconscious infant to the ordinance that its soul might not be lost. Error begets error. One perversion almost always leads to another.

"It is notorious," says Dr. Hodge,* "that the Jewish doctrines of the merit of works, of the necessity and saving efficacy of external rites; of a visible kingdom of Christ of splendor and worldly grandeur; of an external Church out of whose pale there is no salvation; of the priestly character of the ministry; and of a Church hierarchy, soon began to spread among Christians, and at last became ascendant [all which, it may be remarked in passing, was the result of the "Church identity theory"]".

And among other corruptions stood that of infant baptism. Thus stands the rite in the light of history. Here, as in the New Testament Pedobaptism is seen to be of men, springing up with other corruptions, among the wild superstitions of Africa, about the beginning of the *third century.*

"This century," says Dr. Bledsoe,† "suffered, as we learn from historians of the Church, from a decay of learning and the increase of superstition; from the decline of true piety and the growth of priestly arrogance; from an obscuration of divine truth and the inventions of human tradition. In this age, accordingly, the Church reaped a new harvest of errors, the germs of which had been previously planted."

Who would be surprised that such an age, reaping such a harvest of errors, should also reap with the rest, the dogma of Pedobaptism, the germ of which had previously been planted?

---
* Syst. Theol. Vol. III. 738.
† *Southern Review*, April, 1874, p. 348.

Olshausen, after denying that the Scriptures afford any proof-text for infant baptism, thus covers his retreat:*

"Still, however, the propriety of infant baptism is undoubted, and the condition of the Church *after the close of the third century* imperatively required its *introduction.*"

The Doctor seems to think it was *introduced* a little later than the time mentioned by some of his Pedobaptist brethren. That the Church (?) needed something to purge it of its vices and corruptions, no one will deny. But Pedobaptism did not do this. It was simply the *introduction* of another, and a terrible evil, nor did it come alone. What Dr. Bledsoe says of "infant damnation" may be said with equal truth of infant baptism, for they are twin sisters, viz:

"This dogma did not as we may be sure, first show its hideous head amid the advancing lights of learning, religion, and morality. On the contrary, it did, in fact, first appear amid the gathering shadows of ignorance, superstition, and corruption in morals, by which the third century was distinguished from the preceding eras of the Church."†

Such is the much-boasted argument from Church history in favor of infant baptism! Let those, who see fit, practice it because of the weight of the *historical evidence* (?).

But Baptists in rejecting it, stand with De Pressense, of Paris, one of the most learned, as well as one of the most evangelical Pedobaptists of Europe. He says:‡

---
* Comm. Acts xvi. 14, 15.
† *Southern Review*, April, 1874, p. 348.
‡ Ford's Christian Repository, Vol. XII., p. 493.

"This is the great reason [viz: the close connection between *faith* and baptism] why we can not believe that it [Christian baptism] was administered in the apostolic age to little children. No positive fact sanctioning the practice can be adduced from the New Testament; *the historical proofs alleged are in no way conclusive.*" He also says, (as quoted by Dr. Hovey*) "The practice of baptizing the newly born was early introduced into the church, though it does not reach back, in our belief, to the apostolic age.

Such being the admitted facts, how can an intelligent, God-fearing man sprinkle a little water in the face of an unconscious infant, and that too in the sacred name of the Trinity, of the Father, of the Son, and of the Holy Spirit, and call that act Christian baptism? Was there ever a greater misnomer? The question, "Who hath required this at your hands?" ought to startle the Pedobaptist world.

---

* Baptist Quarterly, Vol. IX., p. 138.

CHAPTER X.

The question that has stood before the reader through all these pages, has been answered, *Pedobaptism is of men.* And this work may now be closed. Before doing so, however, it is germane to this question, after the preceding examination of the subject, to state, that against the dogma of infant baptism, quite a number of very serious *charges* can be preferred and sustained. And it is in every sense, pertinent to ask: Is it reasonable to suppose that any practice, even liable to *such charges*, can be of divine appointment? When you have read the charges, then answer as in the sight of God.

Charge 1st. The reader of these pages will readily anticipate the first charge, viz: Pedobaptism is unsupported by the teachings of the New Testament. This is certainly a most serious charge; and until relieved from it, the advocates of infant baptism should not ask an intelligent person to believe the doctrine to be from heaven. That the charge is true will not be doubted by the unbiased reader either of the New Testament, of Church history, or of the baptismal controversy.

If the rite were of divine appointment, one would

naturally expect to find it taught in and supported by the New Testament. For the *whole law*, by which the followers of Christ are to be governed in observing his ordinances, is contained in that book. If you ask, who were to be circumcised; or who admitted to the feast of the passover—or to any of the Jewish rites; at once you would be referred to the *Old* Testament, for all of these are Old Testament ordinances. And there, the law is recorded that regulated them. If you ask, by what authority baptism and the Supper are administered; and to whom they are to be given—for the *whole* law regulating these two ordinances, you are referred at once, not to the *Old*, but to the *New* Testament. Because *both of these* are New Testament ordinances, ordained by Jesus Christ. And *all of his will* concerning them is written in that book. Do you desire to know *Christ's will*, then you must go to *Christ's law*, recorded *exclusively*, but fully, in the New Testament. Now if it was *his will*, that the unintelligent babe should be admitted to baptism and the Supper—the only two ordinances given to his followers—would he not have so commanded? And where but in the *New Testament* would that command be recorded? Or if Christ had designed that the infants should not partake of the Supper, as they did of the Jewish passover, but that they must be admitted to the ordinance of baptism, would he not have so specified, and not left his disciples in the dark concerning these ordinances? And is there *any other* book to which appeal may be made to learn *Christ's will*, except the *New* Testament? Or will *any other book* tell you, with infallible correctness, what *Christ* has commanded concerning his ordinances? If he had appointed *infant* baptism, as he did that of believers, ought it not to be—*would it not have been*—taught *in the New Testament*, the WHOLE *of Christ's revealed will,* just as believer's baptism is taught there?

And is it not true, therefore, that if infant baptism is of divine appointment, *it must be supported by the New Testament?* Upon every question concerning the two ordinances instituted by the Lord Jesus Christ, we are necessarily shut up to the authority of that one book—that book of inspiration, the last will and testament of our dying Lord.

Here and here alone can a man know the commandments of Christ. And here every man, desiring to know them, can do so. They are written so plainly that he that runs may read. And now is it not a very bad omen, a grievous charge, against the practice—that *infant baptism is not supported by the teachings of that book—the book that contains all of Christ's commands concerning his ordinances?*

That this charge is true is proved by what has already been written. But this much additional evidence will be given, and then let him doubt it who can.

(1.) *If it is the duty of the followers of Christ, to have their children baptized, then it is a duty, which they could never learn from the most careful reading of the New Testament.* This can not be denied, for there is "not *one word* in favor of infant baptism" in all its pages.

Would *you* suppose that our Redeemer, as well as our Master, would impose upon his disciples a duty, and hold them responsible for its performance, although he left not one written law concerning the matter? How is the parent to know that it is a duty? Must only the male child, or children of both sexes, be baptized? Are they to be baptized at birth, or on the eighth day thereafter, or at what age? *Where is the law on this matter?* What has Christ commanded concerning it? *It can never be known from the New Testament.*

A converted man, rejoicing in the hope of the glory of God, would learn from *that book*, that he must be baptized; must unite himself to the people of God; must partake of the Lord's Supper; must endeavor to bring others to Christ; would in fact learn *every duty* imposed upon him by the Lord Jesus Christ. But he would never learn from its teachings that he must have his children baptized, for there is not such an *intimation* from the beginning to the end of the book. There can be no obligation, unless there be something upon which it may rest, and on account of which it is obligatory. It is obligatory upon believers to be baptized, *solely* because Christ has so commanded. But why is it obligatory upon a parent to have the child baptized? Christ never commanded it. There is not one word about it in the New Testament. The parent will never learn from reading *that book*, though it contains his whole duty to himself, to his family, and to Christ, that it has been imposed upon him to baptize his infant. Why is it a duty? Why is it obligatory upon Christ's disciples and not on other people? The Pedobaptist world may answer. The late Rev. N. M. Crawford, who during his lifetime was President of more than one college, was raised a Presbyterian. He was united in marriage with a Baptist lady. When his first child was born, he desired, according to the creed of his Church, to have him baptized. But being, as he always was, controlled simply by principle, he determined not to ask his wife to sacrifice her principles, until he could show her a *command* from Christ, *making it obligatory upon him* to have the child sprinkled. A noble resolve indeed, and one worthy of all imitation! Telling her nothing of his feeling, he took his English Testament and read it through carefully, and then reread it. Not a little surprised at his failure to find there the command, and being a good Greek scholar, he turned to his Greek Testament, and gave that a most diligent perusal. But failed utterly to find a single trace of infant baptism. The simple question with him was—Has Christ *required* me to have my child baptized? To this he found no response in the New Testament—Christ's written law—given for our guidance. Any one knowing Dr. Crawford could easily tell what the result would be. He determined, like an honest man, to abandon the practice, and also the Church that taught it, although the Church of his fathers; and very much to the surprise as well as to the joy of his wife, he announced to her one

Sabbath morning his purpose, to unite, on that very day, with the Baptist Church. No doubt there are many, who, like this great and good man, suppose it obligatory upon them to "consecrate their children to the Lord in this way;" and who like him also, up to that time, have never examined the ground of its obligation. What would be the result on Pedobaptism, if parents would not offer their children for baptism, until they had presented to them a *command from Christ* requiring it at their hands? By the authority of the New Testament, a man may preach the Gospel to every creature; baptize them that believe; administer the Lord's Supper to baptized believers; but never can he sprinkle an infant by the authority of that inspired volume.

(2.) *Appeal is also made in sustaining this charge, to your own personal reading of the New Testament.*

You know, as well as any one, that in all that book there is not one word about infant baptism. Of course it is presumed you have read the book, or you would not be talking about what it contains. And *your testimony* must sustain the charge. If you refer to the fact of Christ's blessing little children; to the commission; or to the household baptisms, or to any of those texts sometimes quoted in favor of the practice; you must then be asked to reread what has been written in the preceding pages on those passages. If you refer to the "identity of the churches," and to "baptism in the room of circumcision"—then you must be reminded that those very arguments, considered strong pillars to the cause of infant baptism, have crumbled and fallen before the simple statement of facts that none could dispute. And besides the charge is, that it is unsupported by the *New Testament*.

Can *you* name the book, the chapter and the verse, in *that* portion of God's Word, where infant baptism is even mentioned, to say nothing of *commanded*, and made binding on Christ's disciples? If you can, then stand up boldly for your cause. And if you can not, then most earnestly are you entreated, for the sake of truth, to abandon it, whatever be the consequences, as Crawford, and Campbell, and Judson, and other honored men have done.

(3.) *But appeal is further made to the conduct of the advocates of the dogma, in making their defense.*

Do they defend their cause as if it was supported by the New Testament? No. They will not risk their cause upon this inspired volume—the very one, and the only one to which appeal can be made, and that can give any authority on the subject. Is there a Pedobaptist who is willing to have his cause tested by the *light of the New Testament*, and will pledge himself to abide the decision of *that book?* They tell us truly that baptism is an ordinance of the *New Testament*, but *not one of them*, by the most learned and diligent search, has ever found the slightest mention or allusion even, to *infant* baptism. Ask them to give their authority for the practice; and forthwith, abandoning the

New Testament, they flee to the "identity of the churches," and the Jewish rite of circumcision—to the Old Testament—to learn who are the subjects of this ordinance of the New Testament! Is not this a singular procedure? Why not point out the place—you can certainly do so if it is there—where Christ commanded the baptism of infants, or the apostles practiced it? And then there will be no need of curiously wrought arguments (?). Those who rely upon the ceremonies of Judaism for the support of their cause, are not a little troubled and embarrassed by meeting such men, of their own number, as Strarck, who says:*

"The connection of infant baptism with circumcision deserves no consideration, since there were physical reasons for circumcising in infancy"

And as Bishop Jeremy Taylor who says:

"For the argument from circumcision, it is invalid from infinite considerations. Figures and types prove nothing, unless a command go along with them, or some expression to signify such to be their purpose."

And many others who speak equally as strong and decided.

Others abandoning the *New Testament*, seek refuge among the wild absurdities, and uncertain superstitions of Church history. When Dr. Wood, of Andover, was quoted as saying:

"It is a plain case that there is no express precept respecting infant baptism in our *Sacred Writings*. *The proof then, that it is a divine institution must be made out in some other way,*"

---
* Howell's Evils of Infant Baptism, p. 21.

the reader was left in amazing wonder no doubt, as to what the "*some other way*," would be, by which an institution would be proved to be divine, after the *whole Bible* had been abandoned. Well, you may have the words of Dr. Wood himself. He says :*

"It can not with any good reason, be denied, or doubted, that those Christian writers, who have, in different ways, given testimony of the prevalence of infant baptism in the *early ages of Christianity*, are credible witnesses. Nor can it be denied that they were under the best advantages to know whether the practice *commenced* in the times of the apostles. On this subject, as they were *not liable to mistake*, so their testimony is entitled to full credit."

This will only provoke a smile from those who read the chapter preceding this one, and remember that these same "*Christian writers*," who "*were not liable to mistake*" (*!*) also called infant *communion* an "*apostolica traditio*." But Dr. Wood, a professor of theology, is satisfied with their testimony —although by it many of the grossest mummeries of Rome could be proved to be divine institutions —and thinks it *sufficient* to support his cause, when the *New Testament*, in fact the *whole of* "*our Sacred Writings*," have utterly failed him, and afford no proof for the dogma.

Others again, such as "Wall, Hammond, and others of that school, claim that *Jewish Proselyte baptism*, is its broad and ample foundation." But Moses Stuart, "Owens, Jennings, and others, *repudiate* Jewish Proselyte baptism," and deny that

---

* Howell's Evils of Infant Baptism, p. 26.

such a thing was known prior to the days of John the Baptist. It is very plain that we *must look* not to Judaism, not to Jewish Proselyte baptism (even if there was such a thing), not to Church history, (which is extremely uncertain), *but to the* NEW TESTAMENT EXCLUSIVELY, to know who are the subjects of Christian baptism, for it is "a New Testament ordinance." And yet the advocates of infant baptism admit willingly the silence of this book concerning the rite. Why talk of the "identity of the churches," of "circumcision replaced by baptism," "Jewish Proselyte baptism," or of "Church history," as the main stay and support of infant baptism, *were it not that the dogma is wholly unsupported by the New Testament?* "By their fruit ye shall know them." Their actions betray their cause and sustain the charge made against it. By their own words they stand condemned.

(4) *But, in sustaining this charge preferred against Pedobaptism, viz: that it is unsupported by the New Testament—appeal is made, finally, to the testimony of Pedobaptist scholars and critics.*

In addition to that already given,* the following will now be presented. John Calvin testifies:

"It is nowhere expressly mentioned *by the evangelists*, that any child was by the apostles baptized."

Neander also testifies :†

"As baptism was closely united with a conscious entrance

---

* See Chapters IV. and VI. *et al* of this work.
† Both Calvin and Neander are quoted from Howell's Evil of Infant Baptism, p. 21.

on Christian communion, *faith and baptism were always connected with one another;* and thus it is in the highest degree probable that baptism was performed *only in instances where both could meet together, and that the practice of infant baptism was unknown* " to the apostolic age.

By this time the reader is familiar with the name of Dr. Bledsoe. His testimony is valuable, because of his standing as an able Methodist divine; because it is of recent date; and because his *Review* is published *now* under the auspices of the M. E. Church, South, having received a fresh indorsement from the last General Conference of that Church, held in Louisville, May 1874.* After conceding

" With all our searching, we have been unable to find in the New Testament, a single express declaration, *or word* in favor of infant baptism;" and declaring that " Hundreds of learned Pedobaptists have come to the same conclusion; *especially* since the New Testament has been subject to a closer, a more conscientious, and more candid exegesis, than was formerly practiced;"

Dr. Bledsoe cited in corroboration of his statement, the following distinguished advocates of the practice :†

"In Knapp's Theology, for example it is said : ' There is no decisive example for this practice in the New Testament; for it may be objected against those passages where the baptism of whole families is mentioned, viz: Acts x. 42–48; xvi. 15–33; 1 Corinthians i. 16—that it is doubtful whether there were any children in those families, and if they were, whether they were then baptized. From the passage, Matthew xxviii. 19, it does not necessarily follow that Christ commanded infant baptism (the *matheteuine* is neither

---

* The month AFTER he published his *sweeping* concession. This is significant.

† *Southern Review*, April, 1874, pp. 334, 335.

for or against); nor does this follow any more from John iii. 5, and Mark x. 14–16. *There is therefore no express command for infant baptism in the New Testament*, as Morus (p. 215) justly concedes.' (Vol. II. p. 524). Dr. Jacobi says: ' However reasonably we may be convinced that we find in the Christian Scriptures "the fundamental idea from which infant baptism was *afterward developed*," and by which it may now be justified, it ought to be distinctly acknowledged that it is not an apostolic ordinance.' (p. 271)."

To this Dr. Bledsoe adds the testimony of Neander, and then assures his reader of the abundance of such testimony in the following strong terms:

"We might, if necessary, adduce the admission of *many other profoundly learned Pedobaptists, that their doctrine is not found in the* NEW TESTAMENT, EITHER IN EXPRESS TERMS, OR BY IMPLICATION FROM ANY PORTION OF ITS LANGUAGE." (Emphasis mine.)

Very good testimony this, to sustain the charge preferred! But this is not all. When by some of his Methodist brethren, Dr. Bledsoe was called to an account for these sweeping concessions, in the very next issue of his *Review** he responded as follows:

"Mr. Miller is unduly alarmed at our honest admission that there is no *express command* [his admission was stronger than that] for infant baptism in the New Testament. He seems to think, indeed, that this admission ruins the cause of infant baptism. If so, then it was ruined by *Watson*, and *Wesley*, and *Knapp* and *Jacobi*, long before we ever alluded to the subject. Nor is this all; *for almost all writers in favor of infant baptism have made precisely the same admission.*"

It is no marvel that Mr. Miller, should, before

---
* For July, p. 177.

such concessions, tremble for his cause! But as Mr. Miller can not help the matter, he only relieves himself by saying of Dr. B.'s position :*

"The absurd and self-annihilating and contradictory attitude of a man who deliberately administers a rite in the name of Jesus Christ, for which Christ never uttered one word, renders that opinion [viz: that the baptism of young children is to be retained in the Church, although there is not one word in the New Testament in its favor] in this case, simply nugatory."

THAT IS TRUE. But it is the condition of the whole Pedobaptist world. In two things they agree, viz: That baptism is a New Testament ordinance, ordained by Jesus Christ; and that Christ and his apostles—*the writings of the New Testament—are silent* about *infant* baptism. They "are constrained to confess that *infants* and *baptism* are distinct words, and nowhere joined together in the *New Testament*. God has put them asunder." And what God hath put asunder let no man join together.

Has not the charge—*Pedobaptism is unsupported by the New Testament*—been amply sustained, even by the testimony of its friends? The *New* Testament teaches us our whole duty, but says nothing in favor of infant baptism. Dear reader, are you willing to practice, or to sustain by your words, or by your membership even to countenance what is not sustained by the New Testament? Will you sanction what neither your Master nor his apostles sanctioned? Will you thus venture to

---

* Quoted in *Review* for July, 1874, p. 173.

trifle with the Word of God? Read what he says and take warning. "What thing soever *I* command you, observe to do it. *Thou shalt not add thereto*, nor diminish from it." It is a fearful thing to tamper with the word of the Lord. Has he commanded infants to be baptized? If so, it *must* be done. If not, who will dare to do it, in his name?

This one charge sustained, is sufficient to condemn the cause.

A few others, however, will be—must be *briefly* —given. But until Pedobaptists can relieve their cause of *this one*, they should hold their peace— *imitate the silence of the New Testament*—"the supreme standard by which all human conduct, creeds and opinions should be tried."

CHARGE 2D. PEDOBAPTISM CONTRAVENES THE COMMAND OF CHRIST TO BAPTIZE BELIEVERS.

The constant and the inevitable tendency of infant baptism is to do away with believer's baptism. That this latter is of divine appointment is universally admitted. Can any one believe that Christ is the author of two ordinances, between which there is an inevitable and irreconcilable antagonism? Would he appoint two ordinances, any more than he would create two systems of worlds, that would always antagonize, each the other? Verily not. There is perfect harmony in all of his works and appointments. Let Pedobaptism prevail universally, and in a short time believer's baptism would be a thing of the past. But for the faithfulness of Baptists in ages past, there would be no such thing as believer's baptism to-day. Between the two there is a positive and a direct conflict. One of them therefore can not be of divine appointment—unless God be made the author of confusion. If this human rite should prevail, then believer's baptism, an ordinance established and perpetuated by Christ to be observed "always, even to the end of the world," would be abolished. There would be no Gospel baptism on earth; but only a human rite, meaningless in the extreme. When any system, or ordinance, in any way, contravenes the teachings of the New Testament, or its ordinances, either in design, or action, or subject; that system or ordinance, whatever else it may have in its favor, must be stamped as false, as not of divine appointment. Such is the case with this rite. Ever since it was first introduced into the world, about the beginning of the third century, it has run counter to the commands of God as recorded in the New Testament, contravening and vitiating the ordinances of Christ, as well as his Church, and "the faith once delivered to the saints." It can not, therefore, be of divine appointment. Pedobaptism is "a human tradition arraying itself in deadly hostility to an ordinance of heaven, and attempting with all the energy of desperation, to destroy it and leave no memorial of its existence on the face of the globe." To preserve the ordinances of Christ in their purity ought to be the faithful endeavor of all his followers.

God desires that his people—in fact he claims only those as his people who—"*walk* in his statutes, and *keep* his *ordinances* and do them." And the inspired man of God wrote to his brethren at Corinth: "Now I praise you, brethren, that ye remember me in all things, and *keep the ordinances*, as I delivered them unto you." The Savior has commanded to baptize believers—this is his ordinance, believer's baptism. Infant baptism has been introduced by men in opposition to this. Our Redeemer presses his disciples with the stirring words, "If ye love me, keep my commandments." Let all who *love him and desire to obey him*, say whether *Pedobaptism* shall not rather be abolished. Blessed Master, give us grace to do, in all things, as thou hast commanded!

CHARGE 3D. PEDOBAPTISM HAS BEEN THE CAUSE OF A VAST DEAL OF THE FIERCEST PERSECUTION, THAT HAS EVER BEEN WAGED AGAINST THE FOLLOWERS OF JESUS.

The Baptists, who are of such power in this land, numbering now *largely over one and one-half million* of members, with their numerous Schools, and Seminaries, and Colleges, are a most ancient people. Antedating the rise of the various Protestant denominations, which took place either at the same time with, or since, the great Reformation of the sixteenth century, the Baptists have never been traced to their origin, except as they have been traced back to the days of the apostles. And then, the historian must depend almost solely upon the testimony given by their enemies. By the following quotations their antiquity is made manifest.

Dr. Mosheim, a learned Pedoboptist historian, in his history of the Anabaptists (p. 490–1.) says:*

---

* Quoted in Ford's Origin of the Baptists, pp. 52, 53.

"The true origin of that sect which acquired the denomination of Anabaptists, by their administering anew the rite of baptism to those who came over to their communion, and derive that of Mennonites, from that famous man to whom they owe much of their present felicity, is *hidden in the depths of antiquity*, and is of consequence difficult to be ascertained. This uncertainty will not appear surprising when it is considered that this sect [Anabaptists or Baptists] started up suddenly in several countries at the same point of time, under leaders of different talents and different intentions, and at the very period when the first contests of the Reformers with the Roman Pontiffs drew the attention of the world, and employed all the pens of the learned in such a manner as to render all other objects and incidents almost matters of indifference." [The Anabaptists] "not only considered themselves descendants of the Waldenses, who were so grievously oppressed and persecuted by the despotic heads of the Romish Church, but pretend, moreover, to be the purest offspring of the respectable sufferers, being equally opposed to all principles of rebellion on the one hand, and all suggestions of fanatacisms on the other." "It may be observed," continues this enemy of the Baptists, "that they are not entirely in an error when they boast of their descent from the Waldenses, Petrobanssians, and other *ancient sects*, who are usually considered as witnesses of the truth in times of general darkness and superstition. *Before the rise of Luther and Calvin*, there lay concealed in almost all the countries of Europe, particularly in Bohemia, Moravia, Switzerland, and Germany, many persons who adhered tenaciously to the doctrine, etc., which is the true source of all the peculiarities which are to be found in the religious doctrine and discipline of the Anabaptists."

In 1819, the King of Holland appointed Dr. Ypeij, professor of theology in the University at Groningen, and Rev. J. J. Dermont, chaplain to the king, both of them learned Pedobaptists of the Dutch Reformed Church, to prepare a history of their Church. In their history, they devote one chapter to the Baptists, in which they make the following statement concerning them:*

"We have now seen that the Baptists who were formerly called Anabaptists, and, in latter times, Mennonites, were the original Waldenses; and who have long, in the history of the Church, received the honor of that origin. *On this account*, THE BAPTISTS MAY BE CONSIDERED AS THE ONLY CHRISTIAN COMMUNITY WHICH HAS STOOD SINCE THE DAYS OF THE APOSTLES, AND AS A CHRISTIAN SOCIETY, WHICH HAS PRESERVED PURE THE DOCTRINES OF THE GOSPEL THROUGH ALL AGES. The perfectly correct external and internal economy of the Baptist denomination, tends to confirm the truth, disputed by the Romish Church, that the Reformation brought about in the sixteenth century, was in the highest degree necessary; and at the same time goes to refute the erroneous notion of the Catholics, that their communion is the most ancient."

Dr. Brown well says:

"This testimony, from the highest official authority in the Dutch Reformed Church, is certainly a rare instance of liberality towards another denomination."

And pretty good testimony is this to the apostolic origin of the Baptists, especially as it comes from men who are not Baptists but are faithful and competent historians.

Alexander Campbell says:†

"Clouds of witnesses attest the fact, *that before the Reformation from Popery, and from the apostolic age to the present time*, the sentiments of Baptists, and the practice of baptism have had a continued chain of advocates, and public monuments of their existence in every century can be produced."

But the history of this ancient people, whose

---

* Ency. Relig. Knowledge. Art. Mennonites, p. 796.
† Debate with Maccalla, p. 378.

"origin is hidden in the depths of antiquity," has never been written. The Baptists have an unwritten history—one that perhaps can not be written except in the light of eternity.

Their history faithfully and fully written, would be a history, to a large degree, of the suffering, of the persecutions, and of the cruel deaths, which have been inflicted upon the followers of Jesus, because of their fidelity to him and their steadfastness in " the faith once delivered to the saints." In all the ages Baptists have suffered persecutions by fires, imprisonment, torture by the inquisition, scourging, and martyrdom—they "had trials of cruel mockings and scourgings, yea, moreover, of bonds and imprisonment: they were stoned, they were sawn asunder, were tempted, were slain with the sword: they wandered about in sheepskins and and goatskins; being destitute, afflicted, tormented; of whom the world was not worthy: they wandered in deserts, and in mountains, and in dens and caves of the earth." How true it has been of them, that they who would live godly in this world must suffer persecution! And though they have never once persecuted, yet they have suffered persecution at the hands of nearly every other denomination! And for nothing have these ancient people suffered more than for their firm adherence to believer's baptism on the one hand, and for their constant and persistent opposition to infant baptism on the other. Since its introduction into the world Baptists have ever raised their voices against the human invention. Often when they have been burned, or put to the rack, or persecuted in many ways, the whole of their offense has been their opposition to infant baptism.

The time has been when if a minister wrote or spoke against the rite, he did it knowing that he must suffer—when, if such a book as this was written, the writer must pay for the deed by burning at the stake.

Trace them through all their persecution and you will find that the secondary if not the prime cause of their persecution was their opposition to infant baptism. To prove this by the production of facts is not necessary. Its truthfulness is too well and too sadly known to every reader of Church history. Says Mr. Motley* of the Council of Troubles, called also the Bloody Council, over which the Duke of Alva presided in the Netherlands:

"So well did this new and terrible engine perform its work, that in less than three months from the time of its erection, *eighteen hundred* human beings (or twenty a day) had suffered death by its summary proceedings; some of the highest, the noblest, and the most virtuous in the land among the number; *nor had it then manifested the slightest indication of faltering in its dread career.*"

"Upon the 16th of February, 1568, a sentence of the Holy Office condemned *all the inhabitants* of the Netherlands *to death* as heretics. From this universal doom, *only a few persons, specially named*, were excepted. A proclamation of the king, dated ten days later, confirmed this decree, and ordered it to be carried into instant execution, without regard to age, sex, or condition. This is probably the most concise death-warrant that was ever framed. THREE MILLIONS OF PEOPLE, *men, women and children, were sentenced to the scaffold* IN THREE LINES."

---

* Hovey's Tract on Evils of Infant Baptism, p. 47.

And this for heresy. (See Dr. Hovey's tract.) The massacre of St. Bartholomew need not be mentioned, which occurred in France, August 24, 1572, and lasted thirty days; during which time *thirty thousand persons were put to death* (ONE THOUSAND PER DAY!) The climax is terrible. Thus they suffered by "confiscation, banishment, the dungeon, the rack, for a clear conscience and a pure life! In [Virginia and] New England, in Old England, in and throughout Europe! with now and then a Duke of Alva or a St. Bartholomew massacre!"

What a record against Pedobaptism! Behold! oh, ye, who defend the dogma, what it has produced to the followers of Jesus! This is the fruit of your most favored tree! "It will never be known till the revelations of the last day, what multitudes have been put to death for denying the right of the unconscious infants to the ordinance of baptism. O Babylon! drunken with the blood of the saints and the martyrs of Jesus, a fearful doom awaits thee! During the dark ages the spirit that prompted Augustine and his coadjutors to anathematize the opposers of infant baptism, prevailed, and became intensely rancorous. Could the martyred Paulicians, Waldenses, and Albigenses rise from the dead, they would tell a tale that would send a thrill of horror through the heart of humanity." But let the curtain fall; and hide this dark picture from sight. Let Pedobaptists turn away and cover themselves in sackcloth and in ashes!!

CHARGE 4TH. PEDOBAPTISM IS UTTERLY SUBVERSIVE

OF THE PURITY AND THE SPIRITUALITY OF THE CHURCH OF CHRIST.

A regenerated membership is the motto, and the only safeguard of the spiritual character of Christ's Church.

Nothing can fit an individual for membership in a Church of Christ, except *regeneration.* Let this be absent and nothing else will suffice. And surely if we have any concern for its purity, and for apostolic example, nothing less can be demanded as a prerequisite to church-membership, and admittance to the ordinances of the Lord's house, *than a profession of faith in Christ,* which always implies or presupposes a previous birth of the Spirit. For, "Whosoever believeth that Jesus is the Christ is born of God."*

The man who renders acceptable obedience to Christ, in keeping his commandments, is the man who loves Christ. "He that hath my commandments, and keepeth them, he it is that loveth me."† And yet "every one that loveth is born of God, and knoweth God."‡ And no one can enjoy the worship, the spiritual service of the sanctuary, except he have the birth from on high—or regeneration wrought by the Holy Spirit. How emphatic are the words of the Savior, "Verily, verily, I say unto thee, except a man be born again [*i. e.,* from *above*; 'born, not of blood, nor of the will of the flesh, nor of the will of man, but of God'], he can not see the kingdom of God."§ "Marvel not that

---

* 1 John v. 1. † John xiv. 21. ‡ 1 John iv. 7.
§ John iii. 8 and i. 18.

I said unto thee, ye *must be born from above.*" The apostolic churches grew rapidly. But their increase were additions made by the Lord. "The *Lord* added to the Church daily, *those who are saved.*"* Paul planted and Apollos watered, " but *God gave the increase.*"† The Lord has always been the builder of his spiritual temple and he puts in no material but that which is spiritual—or which is born of the Spirit, for only "that which is born of the Spirit is spirit," or spiritual.

Hence the peculiar terms in which the apostolic churches were addressed in the Epistles. And such is the description also of those churches by inspired men. "And such [*i. e.*, as he had described above; persons of the most degraded character; now, before you were the subject of New Birth, such] were some of you; but ye are washed, but ye are sanctified, but ye are justified in the name of the Lord Jesus, and by the Spirit of our God."‡

"Ye also, as lively stones, are built up a spiritual house, a holy priesthood, to offer up spiritual sacrifices, acceptable to God by Jesus Christ * * * Ye are a chosen generation, a royal priesthood, a holy nation, a peculiar people; that ye should show forth the praises of him who hath called you out of darkness into his marvelous light."§ Such is the inspired description of the *character* and of the design of Christ's Church. But how utterly inappropriate and averse is every word in this description to Pedobaptism—a system " which justifies the

---

* Acts ii. 47.   † 1 Cor. iii. 6, 7.   ‡ 1 Cor. vi. 9, 10, 11.
§ 1 Peter ii. 5, 9, 10, 11.

deliberate introduction of unbelievers into the family of believers, the deliberate placing of other than 'living stones' in the building of God." Read again the apostolic declarations of the material of which the Church is composed. Could such things be said of Pedobaptist churches into which are received *unregenerated* infants, *unregenerated* seekers, and *unregenerated* penitents? Can such persons be designated as "lively stones," or a "spiritual house," etc.? Can they "offer up spiritual sacrifices?" Can they "show forth the praises of God?" Have they been "called out of darkness into his marvelous light?" While by divine appointment Christ's Church, like Solomon's temple, is to be built of material prepared and made ready before it is brought hither, and thus be preserved in its purity, yet, if infant baptism was the rule, many who are unregenerated, many who are the most immoral and the basest members of society, would be introduced into the Church. Such a course would obliterate, entirely and forever, every trace of the line of demarkation between the world and the Church. *They would be one.* The unregenerated part would soon have the ascendency, and then what would become of the purity and the spirituality of the churches? There would be either no Church, or no world, or a Church most intensely worldly in its nature.

Pedobaptism, even with its present strictures and opposition, has greatly marred the beauty of Zion. Infant baptism and a regenerated church-membership are as irreconcilable as light and darkness. The latter is our only safeguard. Admit the former, and you make a gap in the wall through which the Church will be deluged with such corruption and vice, superstition and perversion of the truth, as characterized the "dark ages." Christianity has never known a more blighting or a more corrupting curse than the adulterous union of Church and State. And of this Pedobaptism is the foundation-stone; and is justly chargeable with all the evils and miseries which have been entailed upon the Church, and upon humanity, by such an adulterous union. These have been most numerous and most terrible, and some of them most diabolical. By Pedobaptism the Church of Christ is shorn of its chiefest glory; and the right arm of its power is broken!

CHARGE 5TH. BY IT, THE CHILD IS ROBBED OF ITS PRIVILEGE AND HINDERED IN ITS DUTY OF RENDERING PERSONAL OBEDIENCE TO THE SAVIOR, AND, THEREFORE, OF HAVING THE ANSWER OF A GOOD CONSCIENCE TOWARD GOD IN BAPTISM.

It is sometimes said, when all other arguments have failed to satisfy the conscience: "If the baptism of infants does no good, it certainly will do no harm." But this is not the question. Did Christ command you to baptize children, or to have your child baptized? If so, then by all means do it. But where has he given the command? Not in the New Testament surely. *It is a sin* to do anything in the name of Christ, about which Christ never uttered one word. And besides, the statement is by no means true. For it does harm—and a great harm at that—to admit infants to the ordinance of Christian baptism. It does harm to the Church, to the minister, to the teachings of the Bible, to the parents of the child, and especially to the child itself. It works mischief all around.

Though Christ commanded *all* believers to be baptized, yet that child, having grown up, and believed on Christ, lives—must, by the work and vows of the parent, live—in open disobedience to his Savior's command. Is this a small matter? It is worse than nonsense to talk of the child, on coming to riper years, adopting the act of the parent as its own individual act. The child knew nothing of it. And never can the act be so received by the child, as to become the child's *own personal obedience* in the sight of God. Religion is strictly a *personal matter*. *Each one* has to do with God for himself. Every one must repent for himself; must believe for himself; must love, and must render *personal obedience* for himself, as well as give an account unto God for himself. This last would not be true, if the former things were not true also. They are inseparably linked together. A person is responsible, and will be called to give account, only for his conduct in respect to *personal duties*, which God has imposed upon him, or required at his hands. All of the above mentioned things God has required of *each individual* for himself, they are *personal duties;* and therefore, "*every one* of us shall give account of *himself* to God."[*] But those baptized in infancy can never

---

[*] Rom. xiv. 12.

render a *personal obedience* to Christ in baptism. As they have lived, so they must die, and go to judgment without having obeyed the command—the last, parting command—given by their Savior just before he ascended to the throne of his glory. Is all this no harm? Nor can they ever enjoy the approval of a good conscience toward God. Their conscience will never be satisfied that its demands have been met, unless peradventure, it be as badly perverted as was the conscience of Saul of Tarsus, who verily thought he did God service in persecuting the Church of Christ.

Oh, parents, will you not be entreated in behalf of your children?

Will you still continue to impose upon them, in the solemn name of the Triune God, an ordinance meaningless in all its parts, and without any sanction whatever in the Word of God? Is it not a fearful and a dangerous procedure?

Are you willing to rob your children of the blessedness of having their conscience satisfied, and bear them witness in the Holy Spirit that they have rendered unto God all his requirements? Are you willing to deprive your children of the highest joy known to a believer in the Lord Jesus Christ while on earth, viz: the joy found in keeping the commandments of him who loved us and gave himself for us? All this you do, and more besides, every time you have one of your children sprinkled.

And if any, baptized in infancy, should read these pages, will you suffer one *personal* question to be put to you—and it is asked in all tenderness and kindness of heart. You must admit, that, whatever your parents did for you, yet *you* have not obeyed Christ for *yourself*. Are *you* willing to meet your Redeemer in heaven—in death and at the judgment—after slighting and neglecting, for a whole lifetime, the *last commandment* he left on record for you, viz: be baptized?

CHARGE 6TH. PEDOBAPTISM IS FOUNDED IN PRINCIPLES, WHICH STRIKE AT THE VERY FOUNDATION OF THE GREAT AND FUNDAMENTAL DOCTRINES OF THE SCHEME OF REDEMPTION.

"A fundamental misconception of the truth of the Gospel, gave it birth, while misapprehension of the teachings of the New Testament prolongs its disastrous existence."

The doctrine of universal depravity; the great fundamental doctrine of justification by faith; the doctrine of the agency of the Holy Spirit in regeneration; the Scripture doctrine of infant salvation; the true principle of civil and religious liberty; the union of believers for which Christ prayed; the Scriptural design, and the wonderful significance of Christian baptism; all of these, and others that could be mentioned of the great doctrines of the economy of grace, are either contradicted, antagonized, falsified, perverted, or wholly overthrown by the dogma of infant baptism. To elaborate this charge to its fullest extent would require a volume. This then can not be done here. The charge has been made, that Baptists have caused and prolonged the divisions among Christians. But from the very nature of things this can not be true. They offer a broader and a more ample and just basis of Christian union than any other denomination. Nearly every article of their faith—especially those on the subjects about which there are divisions—is believed by nearly all the Protestant denominations. They accept our Creed, but desire to make additions it is, just as they do to the New Testament.

What is accepted and held by all can never cause division. None of their articles of faith, therefore, are schismatical. Baptists believe that the immersion in water of a proper subject in the name of the Trinity is Christian baptism. But this article of faith does not belong exclusively to them. It is accepted and considered baptism by all Christendom. To hold to *immersion* as baptism can never therefore cause division. But to the point in hand.

Baptists hold that a *believer* in the Lord Jesus Christ, is a Scriptural and therefore a fit subject for Christian baptism. And no one denies it, who believes in water baptism at all. It is universally accepted as true, as sanctioned or authorized in the Word of God. *Believer's baptism*—like immersion—*passes everywhere.*

There can be no divisions, therefore, on account of this doctrine. Why then are Christ's followers divided? Not for anything held by Baptists touching this doctrine; but here is the entering and the dividing wedge—"*and their children.*" And who made this wedge? And who inserts it and drives it until the people of God are rent asunder? Is it the work of Baptists, or of Pedobaptists? The answer is easy. There is just as much in the Creed of every Baptist Church, "in favor of infant baptism," as there is in the Word of God, *i. e.*," *not one word,*" "not a single trace," etc. It is the dogma of Pedobaptism that divides the followers of Christ.

Again: It is opposed to the work of the Holy Spirit. The Rev. Wm. Bates, Lecturer of Christ's College, Cambridge, in "College Lectures on Christian Antiquities and the Rituals," p. 399, propounds the following question and answer :*

"Why must parents and friends be careful to get their children baptized?" Because by this ordinance their original sin is washed away and they are grafted into the body of Christ."

John Wesley, the founder of the Methodist Church, also said:†

"If infants are guilty of original sin, then they are proper subjects of baptism; seeing, in the ordinary way, *they can not be saved, unless this be washed away by baptism.*"

In the *advertisement* of this book, "published by order of the General Conference," occurs the following sentence or sentences:

"Several of the following tracts were formerly published in the form of Discipline ; but as this undergoes a revision once in four years, the General Conference of 1812 ordered these tracts to be left out of the Discipline; and, that they might still be within reach of every reader, directed them to be published in a separate volume. They have been accordingly prepared and published in this form, in a *stereotyped* edition."

So wholesome is Mr. Wesley's doctrine touching the *washing away of sins by baptism*, in the sight

---

* See Tract on Church Polity, by Dr. Wm. Williams, p. 41.
† *Doctrinal Tracts*, p. 251.

of the Methodists, that they not only heartily indorse it in General Convocation, but circulate it that all may read; and then, to preserve it from the ravages of time, and the influence of a better understanding of God's Word—so destructive to all such errors, they have STEREOTYPED IT. Stereotyped what? Why, that INFANTS "CAN NOT BE SAVED, UNLESS THIS [THEIR ORIGINAL SIN] BE WASHED AWAY BY BAPTISM." Behold, the ruinous effects of Pedobaptism upon the plan of salvation "by grace through faith" as revealed in the Scripture! See how it robs the Holy Spirit of his work; overlooks the Scripture plan of infant salvation; and perverts this sublime ordinance of Christ, in its true significance, beauty, and design? Such are its effects upon the Christian system. To defend or to support in any way the dogma is to strike with heavy blows the central pillar of the truth of the Gospel.

Further the cause of Pedobaptism, and you undermine the very foundation stones of the magnificent temple of the "faith once delivered to the saints;" and that temple, if it does not fall, will be shaken from the tower to its very base. Pedobaptism is at war with every true principle of Christianity. Any *one* of the above charges is sufficient to condemn the rite as of human origin. Others might be given; or either of these could have been further elaborated. And now let an intelligent world, and especially those who love the Savior, decide, with an unprejudiced mind, whether a dogma, against which such charges have been sustained, ought to be defended and practiced as a divine institution. These objections to infant baptism are sufficient to induce all, who bow to the Savior's authority, to enlist under his banner, and to wage a war of extermination against this human rite, contravening Christ's commands, subverting his doctrines, dividing his followers, entailing upon humanity untold miseries, and withal having no sanction in the Word of God.

The words of Prof. Lange, one of the foremost Pedobaptists of Europe, are of the most weighty import; and would that they could be sounded through the length and breadth of the land, that every one who bears the title Pedobaptist might hear them:

"Would the Protestant Church fulfill and attain to its final destiny, *the baptism of new-born children must of necessity be abolished.* It has sunk down to a mere formality, without any meaning for the child."*

---
* Baptist Short Method, p. 120.

CHAPTER XI.

CONCLUSION.

As the present work has already reached, and even gone beyond, the original intentions of the writer, it may seem an encroachment upon the patience of the reader to add anything further. A word or two however must be added in conclusion.

I. And first it is proper *to sum up* what has been done in the preceding pages.

The following propositions (the writer would modestly submit) have been fully established.

(1) Infant baptism was not ordained by Jesus Christ; though Christian baptism is an ordinance of his appointment; (2) The Apostles, in imitation of their Master, nowhere either practiced or mentioned, or even in any way alluded to *infant* baptism, though there are numerous accounts of their administering, in obedience to Christ's command, the ordinance of Christian baptism. They uniformly and exclusively baptized *believers;* (3) The claims so often made to the identity of the Church of Christ and the Jewish Theocracy, and to the substitution of baptism in the room of circumcision, are

wholly gratuitous assumptions, and afford not the slightest support to infant baptism; (4) Through a superstitious perversion of the design of the ordinance of baptism, along with the corruptions of other doctrines so common to the "dark ages," *infant baptism had its origin*, (perhaps among the wild vagaries of benighted Africa, where no apostle, or inspired man, so far as is known, ever preached or labored, but where Cyprian lived as pastor, and taught his mischievous doctrines). And for the first time in all the records of history it is mentioned in the *third century* by Tertullian, who condemned the practice, as having no foundation either in reason or in revelation; (5) To all of the above points many of the ablest Pedobaptists have given the weight of their *most unqualified concessions;* claiming, however, this *silence*—throughout the New Testament, also for *centuries* of uninspired history,—as an argument in favor of the practice. The *profound silence* of *centuries*—of one, two, or three hundred years! How loudly, and eloquently, and withal how *correctly*, especially, it speaks!!

"How wonderful the ear that catches the sounds of silence! How sweet to one, blessed with such a rare possession, must be the music of stillness, echoed by the hills of nonentity! To such persons, of course, the *silenc* of the New Testament is as the voice of many waters in favor of infant baptism."

(6) And against this dogma there are many serious charges, some of which have been preferred and sustained. These points having been established, it is, therefore, evident that infant baptism is not

from heaven, is not of divine appointment; but is an institution of man. No longer should it, therefore, be administered as of divine appointment, but should be abandoned by all lovers of the truth of the Gospel.

II. The following was taken from the *Christian Advocate*, June 5th, 1875, a Methodist paper published in Nashville, Tennessee.

"INFANT BAPTISM."

"In your issue of the 22d you 'call attention to the sad neglect of infant baptism in this country,' and attribute it to 'the decay of piety—family religion.' Allow me to say, in addition to this, that it is, according to my observation for many years past, in a considerable degree, owing to the prevalence of anti-pedobaptism in our Church. You know our rubric allows the candidate the choice of sprinkling, pouring, or immersion, in the mode of baptism, and through this door thousands have been admitted into the Church who are thorough anti-pedobaptists except close communion; and they not only neglect to have their children baptized, but are flatly opposed to it in every sense of the word. While this door stands open, and anti-pedobaptists maintain their exclusive close-communion doctrine and practice, may we not expect it will go on increasing more and more? Another reason for it is, that our pastors in this country do not preach the nature, ground, and duty of infant baptism as much as they ought to do. It is seldom that the subject is introduced in our pulpits, notwithstanding there is an unceasing fire kept up from the line of the opposition.

"T. L. BOSWELL."

That is a wonderful paragraph, coming as it does from the pen of a Methodist, and published in a Methodist paper! Several items might be noticed. The fact that infant baptism is on the decline, as is here asserted, is a matter of great joy to all who rejoice in the simplicity of the truth, and the purity of the ordinances of the Gospel.*

But have not these writers made a mistake in pointing out the cause of that decline? Certainly, the main—the underlying—cause for it, is the increase in New Testament knowledge. Somehow, account for it as you may, where the Bible is fully circulated and read, infant baptism will not thrive.

In fact the masses can not find the rite in "all our sacred writings." And, what is worse, their leaders can neither give them a plain "thus saith the Lord," nor can they give any scriptural reason, for the practice; "especially since," as Dr. Bledsoe said, "the New Testament has been subjected to a

---

* The following bit of information, appearing in the editorial column of *The Religious Herald*, published in Richmond, Virginia, December 2d, 1875, is pertinent to this point.

"DECLINE OF INFANT BAPTISM.

"The Virginia Conference of the Methodist Episcopal Church South was in session week before last in the town of Danville, in this State. From the report of its proceedings in the *Danville News*, copied into the Fredericksburg *Daily News*, we make the following extracts:

"*Madison*—John W. Hildrup. Report good; nothing against him; only one infant baptized. The Bishop wished to know if this was a fair representation of the work in his section.

"*Fluvanna*—Rev. John W. Howard. Report good; nothing against him. The Bishop did not think that the Church was making any headway, if, out of over 500 members, not a single infant baptism. The report of the minister showed that tne best men on his circuit objected to having their children baptized.

"*Bedford*—Edgar H. Pritchett. Reported no infant baptism, which was accounted for by the brother, who stated that it was because there were fewer children this last year.

"*Appomattox*—James E. McSparian. Reported as being in ill health; infant baptism none, stating that it had gone by the board.

" Most of the remaining reports from the circuits and stations, on the day referred to, contained no account of infant baptisms; and in others the number of such baptisms stated varied from two to twelve."

closer, more conscientious, and more candid exegesis, than was formerly practiced." And, further, they can not give to their people *one single* satisfactory reason why they should have their infants baptized. Nor is this in any sense owing to any want of faithful effort on the part of the preachers. They do their *best*. What the writer of the above paragraph says on this point may be true in his immediate neighborhood, but certainly in this State (Kentucky) the opposite is true. A perpetual firing is kept up all along their line.

The preachers have preached on the subject, they have written on it—in periodicals of all sizes, from a weekly county paper up to Bledsoe's Quarterly, in published sermons and in books, and withal they have held debate after debate on the subject. And the conferences have put forth their best men for this special purpose. But the truth is, the more they preach, and the more they write, and, especially, the more they debate, the more infant baptism wanes. And the less inclined are parents to have "the little ones dedicated to God in baptism." The blazing light of God's word is becoming too luminous for the dogma, and it *must* therefore decline. History shows that whenever God's word has been freely circulated and read by the people, the practice of infant baptism has decreased. And when, on the other hand, that word has been chained, or in any way kept from the people, then the dogma revives with all its primeval freshness—for such was its native soil and climate. Nothing is more destructive to this error than Bible knowledge.

The newspaper letter reveals another fact, which no doubt has often been seen and as often wondered at, viz:—"*Thousands* have been admitted into the Church, *who are thorough anti-pedobaptists*—except close communion; and they not only neglect to have their children baptized, *but are flatly opposed to it in every sense of the word.*" This is said only of the Methodists, but it is equally true of all Pedobaptist churches. These persons, it is claimed, remain with these churches, simply because open communion, falsely so called, is practiced in them. But this is impossible unless, peradventure, the persons themselves are woefully and unpardonably ignorant of the Baptist principles of Church Communion. This subject, however, can not be discussed here!* But let one passing remark be made: Baptists are not so close in their communion as are the Pedobaptists. For they will commune with all their own members, while Pedobaptists invariably neglect the infant portion of their membership, and *never* invite them to the table. There is every reason for this as there is for baptizing them. Why are they thus neglected?

These thousands of anti-pedobaptists in Pedobaptist churches have never studied the evil of the dogma of infant baptism—which they however condemn; nor have they ever realized, that the world and all anti-pedobaptists consider them as defending the dogma; that in fact all of their in-

---

* See Gardner's Church Communion.

fluence is in its favor. If they did they certainly could not remain there with an easy conscience. By their membership in these churches they not only countenance, but foster one of the direst evils with which Christianity ever had to deal. Are these thousands willing to lend their support to such an evil? Can they do so and maintain a conscience void of offense before God? Will you be disloyal to Christ, prove traitor to his cause, uphold what you condemn as an error, and an evil, *for any human consideration?* Not unfrequently do we find wives, members in Baptist churches, who, to gratify the whimsical notions of a prejudiced and overbearing husband, go into Pedobaptist churches declaring their opposition to infant baptism. These churches, strange to say, are inconsistent enough to receive them as members in good standing. But can an individual sacrifice their *highest principles* for such a reason? Better die than sacrifice truth. Our fathers have died in opposition to this very error. "Hath the Lord as great delight in burnt-offerings and sacrifices, as in obeying the voice of the Lord? Behold, *to obey* is better than sacrifice, and to hearken than the fat of rams."* And yet intelligent persons talk of being willing to make sacrifices—and that too of things which do not belong to them, for the sake of some family tie—to live in a church with such or such a person. Such persons would do well to *memorize* those cutting words of the Master: "He that loveth father or mother more than me is not worthy of me; and he that loveth son or daughter more than me is not worthy of me. And he that taketh not *his cross* and *followeth after* ME, is not worthy of me."* Christ *first*, in our affections, and, all else afterward. To do his will is our *first* duty. How can a Baptist—a person opposed to infant baptism—live in a Pedobaptist church? Are such churches fit homes for *these thousands of anti-pedobaptists*, who not only neglect to have their children baptized, but are flatly opposed to it in every sense of the word? No. Thrice no. You can not remain there, and be faithful to yourself, faithful to the cause of truth, or faithful to your Master. "Wherefore come out from among them, and be ye separate, saith the Lord, and touch not the unclean thing; and I will receive you, and will be a Father unto you, and ye shall be my sons and daughters, saith the Lord Almighty."†

III. If for the reasons mentioned there are thousands of anti-pedobaptists in Pedobaptist churches, so also are other thousands there, simply because they have never examined the subject for themselves. If they believe it and practice it, they do so either because it is in the creed of their church; or because their parents were raised, and raised them, in that church; and are members not from any well *grounded principles*, but simply by the tide of circumstances. And perhaps some are in, and have not the moral courage to get out, and practice this rite simply because they are in these

---
* Matt. x. 87, 88.
† 2 Cor. vi. 17, 18.

churches. A Presbyterian minister of no mean standing, admitted not long ago to the writer, that he had never examined for himself the question of baptism, either as to its mode or subjects; but he was a Presbyterian simply because his father was. In so saying he but gave utterance to the true feeling and condition of hundreds of his people. Does such a course become any one of Christ's professed followers, to say nothing of one who expounds the law of the Gospel? How would all such reasons vanish as the mist before the morning sun, before the trying persecutions of former ages! Oh! my beloved friend, see that your faith is well founded in the teaching of God's word! And see to it *for yourself*, for "every one of us must give account of himself unto God." Can you render such an account upon the testimony of any one else, even of your parents? Trifle not with the commandments of Christ—for in keeping them there is great reward. But, "be ready always to give an answer to every man that asketh you, a reason of the hope that is in you, with meekness and fear."

IV. Let Baptists be exhorted to remain steadfast to the principles, that have through all the ages, made them a peculiar people.

By unflinching fidelity to these the Baptists have, *under God*, done much for the world, and for the advancement of truth, and toward maintaining the primitive purity and simplicity of the Gospel. While there is no room for *boasting*, yet there is much for which they should be profoundly grateful and humble. The following quotations show something of what Baptists have done, and what they are in the world, even as viewed by those who are not Baptists:

"Let it never be forgotten of the Baptists," said Chalmers,* an eloquent Presbyterian of Scotland, "that they form the denomination of Fuller, and Cary, and Ryland, and Hall, and Foster; that they originated one of all missionary enterprises; that they have enriched the Christian literature of our country with an authorship of the most exalted piety, as well as the first talent, and the first eloquence; that they have waged a noble war with the hydra of Antinomianism; that, perhaps, there is not a more intellectual community of ministers, or who have to their number put forth a greater amount of mental power and mental activity in the defense and illustration of our common faith; and what is still better than all the triumphs of genius and understanding, who by their zeal and fidelity, and pastoral labor among the congregations they have reared, have done more to swell the lists of genuine discipleship in all the walks of private society, and thus both uphold and extend the living Christianity of our nation."

In his work on "Religion in America," Dr. Baird also says:†

"The ministry of the Baptists comprehends a body of men who, in point of talent, learning, and eloquence, as well as devoted piety, have no superiors in the country."

With a great price have they purchased these golden opinions from those who are not of their number! In this country Baptists have grown until they have become a mighty host, "that looketh forth as the morning, fair as the moon, clear as the sun, and terrible as an army with banners." In the

---

* Quoted in Ford's Origin of the Baptists, p. 14.
† As quoted in "What the Baptists have done for the World," a tract by Geo. B. Taylor, D. D., p. 22.

year 1770 there were in the whole United States only seventy-seven Baptist churches. But they have grown and grown until now in the same territory, there are of this once despised and persecuted people, 21,510 churches, 13,354 ministers, and 1,761,171 members. And, while in this State (Kentucky) just one hundred years ago the first Gospel sermon ever preached in the "dark and bloody ground," was preached by a Baptist minister driven from his home in Virginia by persecution; at this time there are in the State, sixty associations, 1,367 churches, 723 ministers, and 147,031 members—one Baptist to every ten of the population. We do not glory in any of these things. "God forbid that we should glory in anything save in the cross of our Lord Jesus Christ." But, oh, *what hath God wrought!* "In the name of our God we lift up our banners," on which are the inscriptions of divine truth—truth that has flamed through all the ages, even in the darkest hours of the darkest nights of superstition; truth that has withstood the ravages of the fiercest persecution, the "TRUTH, LIKE A TORCH, THE MORE 'TIS SHOOK, IT SHINES;" and truth that is written upon this banner by the divine hand and in letters of imperishable light that all may see—

SALVATION BY GRACE THROUGH FAITH;
THE SPIRITUALITY OF CHRIST'S CHURCH;
AND THE ORDINANCES IN THEIR PURITY.

Who would question that *this people*—even the Baptists—have, as Neander said, a future and a future work? Even those who are not of their number are turning to them with kind words of cheer, and with bright expectations. Bishop Smith, of Kentucky, as quoted by Curtis* says:

"God, in his wise Providence, has permitted the rise of the various sects of Baptists for the purpose of ultimately restoring the primitive mode of baptism."

The late Dr. Wood, of Andover, Massachusetts, in 1854, thus expressed himself:†

"I entertain the most cordial esteem, love, and confidence toward the Baptists as a denomination. I have had the freest intercourse, and the sincerest friendship with Baptist ministers, theological students, and private Christians. And I have wished that our denomination—the Congregational—was as free from erratic speculations, and as well founded in the doctrines and experimental principles of the Puritans, as the Baptists. IT SEEMS TO ME THEY ARE THE CHRISTIANS WHO ARE LIKELY TO MAINTAIN PURE CHRISTIANITY, AND TO HOLD FAST THE FORM OF SOUND WORDS."

And Dr. John Hall, a Presbyterian minister of New York, and second to none in his denomination, speaks as follows, touching the tendency to heap censure on the Baptists for their close communion:

"Whether the assailants act wisely or kindly in that matter, or not, is an open question. It is a course of doubtful catholicity to raise a popular cry against a most valuable body of people who honestly defend and consistently go through with what they deem an important principle. 'Charity suffereth long and is kind.' And it is doubtful if, considering the lengths to which liberal ideas have been carried in this country, there be not some gain to the community as a whole from a large denomination making a stand at a particular point and reminding their brethren that there are Church matters which we are not bound, are not

---

* Prog. Bapt. Princ. p. 138.
† See Taylor's tract before referred to, p. 26.

even at liberty, to settle according to the **popular demand,** as we would settle the route of a railroad."

If there was ever a time when Baptists should do their duty, their whole duty, it is now. **Never** through all the ages have they had such an opportunity for spreading their principles—the principles of the Gospel—as they have now. Let Baptists, true to their persecuted ancestry, true to time-honored principles, and above all true to their Master and Redeemer, rise up in the full strength of their manhood. What persecutions, by fires, by confiscations, by scourging, by imprisonment, or by death, could not accomplish, let not the world do by seductive smiles.

Fearlessly defend the truth; and condemn the error. "Contend earnestly for the faith once delivered to the saints;" *but always in a spirit of love and meekness.* While we should love those who differ from us, yet we should love our Savior, his cause, and his truth, more. Through all the ages our fathers have suffered, and died, in contending for these time-honored principles. And shall we, now rejoicing in the work of their hands, surrender the very things for which they have struggled so hard and so long? The Baptist brotherhood, with united breath, all over this land will exclaim— NO, NEVER. We have seen the long train of evil which has resulted from this human institution— of baptizing infants,—are we willing now to turn and smile on it as an angel of purity fresh from the celestial city?

Nurse it, and like a viper it will sting you in return. It is wise to be silent sometimes. But there are times when silence is cowardice—times when to be silent is to be a traitor. Christ has given you his banner, and bid you bear it to the uttermost parts of the earth. Let none mar its beauty. Be true to your orders. Unfurl the banner to the breeze. Move onward, and upward, ever crying for the help and the blessing of your Redeemer—the Captain of your salvation. And never, no never, cease your march until all the kingdoms and nations of this world shall become the kingdoms of our Lord and of his Christ; until *victory!* VICTORY! shall be the cry in every land; "Thanks be unto God who giveth us the victory through our Lord Jesus Chist;" Christ " is KING of kings and LORD of lords."

O God, may the banner which thou hast given to them that fear thee, and upon which is emblazoned the faith of the Gospel, *be displayed* because of the truth!*

Grant thy people grace to say, each one, as thy prophet said: " For Zion's sake I will not hold my peace, and for Jerusalem's sake I will not be silent, until the righteousness thereof go forth as brightness, and the salvation thereof as a lamp that burneth."

---

* Psalm lx. 4.

THE END.

A Biographical Sketch of James Marion Frost (1848-1916)

By
John Franklin Jones

A Biographical Sketch of James Marion Frost (1848-1916)

James Marion Frost—pastor, denominational leader, founder/first secretary of Sunday School Board of the Southern Baptist Convention—was born at Georgetown, Kentucky, February 10, 1848. He graduated from Georgetown College. Frost married Nanney Riley and to that union was born Howard, Margaret, Marian, Marcellus, and Virginius (*ESB*).

He ministered as the pastor of First Baptist, Maysville, Kentucky; Upper Street (now Calvary Baptist), Lexington, Kentucky; First Baptist, Staunton, Virginia; First Baptist Selma, Alabama; Leigh Street Baptist, Richmond, Virginia; and First Baptist, Nashville, Tennessee (*ESB*).

Frost proposed a board of publication to produce literature for the Convention in the *Religious Herald* on February 27, 1890. All the Baptist papers in the various states, excepting those in Tennessee and Kentucky, editorially opposed the resolution. The resolution was considered at the Fort Worth meeting of the Southern Baptist Convention (1890) and a Sunday school committee serving for one year with headquarters in Louisville was appointed ("JMF"). The proposal was adopted in 1891 at the Convention's meeting at Birmingham, Alabama (*ESB*).

After having served only eighteen months and still yearning

for the pastorate, he felt that he could not decline the call to become pastor of the First Baptist Church in Nashville. In 1896, however, he returned to the secretaryship of the board and served in that capacity until his death in 1916 ("JMF"). He developed a graded series of literature, teacher-training programs, developed standards for measuring efficiency of the Sunday school, advocated that Sunday school be closely tied to local churches and the denomination, helped develop Baptist Young People's Union, and began book-publishing during his tenure with the Sunday School Board (*ESB*).

Frost was never physically strong, but he endured twenty-two years of intense administrative pressure in his office at the Sunday School Board. His health gave way en route to a field engagement in 1916. After much suffering ("JMF"), he died at Nashville, Tennessee October 30, 1916 and was buried at Cave Hill Cemetery, Louisville, Kentucky (*ESB*).

Frost authored *Moral Dignity of Baptism* (1905); *The Memorial Supper* (1908); *An Experience of Grace* (1908); *Our Church Life* (1909); *The School and the Church* (1911); and *Sunday School Board History and Work* (1914) (*ESB*).

BIBLIOGRAPHY

Encyclopedia of Southern Baptists. S.v. "Frost, James Marion," by James Sullivan.

"James Marion Frost." Article on-line. Available from http://www.sbhla.org/bio_frost.htm.. Accessed 10 July 2004.

BY JOHN FRANKLIN JONES
CORDOVA, TENNESSEE
JULY 2004

THE BAPTIST STANDARD BEARER, INC.

a non-profit, tax-exempt corporation
committed to the Publication & Preservation
of the Baptist Heritage.

CURRENT TITLES AVAILABLE IN
THE BAPTIST *DISTINCTIVES* SERIES

KIFFIN, WILLIAM   A Sober Discourse of Right to Church-Communion. Wherein is proved by Scripture, the Example of the Primitive Times, and the Practice of All that have Professed the Christian Religion: That no Unbaptized person may be Regularly admitted to the Lord's Supper. (London: George Larkin, 1681).

KINGHORN, JOSEPH   Baptism, A Term of Communion. (Norwich: Bacon, Kinnebrook, and Co., 1816).

KINGHORN, JOSEPH   A Defense of "Baptism, A Term of Communion". In Answer To Robert Hall's Reply. (Norwich: Wilkin and Youngman, 1820).

GILL, JOHN   Gospel Baptism. A Collection of Sermons, Tracts, etc., on Scriptural Authority, the Nature of the New Testament Church and the Ordinance of Baptism by John Gill. (Paris, AR: The Baptist Standard Bearer, Inc., 2006).

CARSON, ALEXANDER	Ecclesiastical Polity of the New Testament. (Dublin: William Carson, 1856).
BOOTH, ABRAHAM	A Defense of the Baptists. A Declaration and Vindication of Three Historically Distinctive Baptist Principles. Compiled and Set Forth in the Republication of Three Books. Revised edition. (Paris, AR: The Baptist Standard Bearer, Inc., 2006).
BOOTH, ABRAHAM	Paedobaptism Examined on the Principles, Concessions, and Reasonings of the Most Learned Paedobaptists. With Replies to the Arguments and Objections of Dr. Williams and Mr. Peter Edwards. 3 volumes. (London: Ebenezer Palmer, 1829).
CARROLL, B. H.	*Ecclesia* - The Church. With an Appendix. (Louisville: Baptist Book Concern, 1903).
CHRISTIAN, JOHN T.	Immersion, The Act of Christian Baptism. (Louisville: Baptist Book Concern, 1891).
FROST, J. M.	Pedobaptism: Is It From Heaven Or Of Men? (Philadelphia: American Baptist Publication Society, 1875).
FULLER, RICHARD	Baptism, and the Terms of Communion; An Argument. (Charleston, SC: Southern Baptist Publication Society, 1854).
GRAVES, J. R.	Tri-Lemma: or, Death By Three Horns. The Presbyterian General Assembly Not Able To Decide This Question: "Is Baptism In The Romish Church Valid?" 1st Edition.

	(Nashville: Southwestern Publishing House, 1861).
MELL, P.H.	Baptism In Its Mode and Subjects. (Charleston, SC: Southern Baptist Publications Society, 1853).
JETER, JEREMIAH B.	Baptist Principles Reset. Consisting of Articles on Distinctive Baptist Principles by Various Authors. With an Appendix. (Richmond: The Religious Herald Co., 1902).
PENDLETON, J.M.	Distinctive Principles of Baptists. (Philadelphia: American Baptist Publication Society, 1882).
THOMAS, JESSE B.	The Church and the Kingdom. A New Testament Study. (Louisville: Baptist Book Concern, 1914).
WALLER, JOHN L.	Open Communion Shown to be Unscriptural & Deleterious. With an introductory essay by Dr. D. R. Campbell and an Appendix. (Louisville: Baptist Book Concern, 1859).

For a complete list of current authors/titles, visit our internet site at:
www.standardbearer.org
or write us at:

he Baptist Standard Bearer, Inc.

NUMBER ONE IRON OAKS DRIVE • PARIS, ARKANSAS 72855

TEL # 479-963-3831   FAX # 479-963-8083

EMAIL: Baptist@centurytel.net   http://www.standardbearer.org

Thou hast given a standard to them that fear thee; that it may be displayed because of the truth. — Psalm 60:4

www.ingramcontent.com/pod-product-compliance
Lightning Source LLC
Chambersburg PA
CBHW031142160426
43193CB00008B/229